Pescatarian Cookbook And Lebanese Food

2 Books In 1: Learn How To Cook Fish And Seafood At Home For Healthy Mediterranean Recipes

Adele Tyler

Lebanese
COOKBOOK

77 Recipes From Lebanon For Traditional
And Easy Dishes With Mediterranean
Flavors

Adele Tyler

Contents

Introduction

Lebanon has food and intellectual intersection, located among eastern and western. The cuisine of Lebanon is unmistakably Mediterranean. Veggies, fruits, organic seafood, and shrimp are in abundance, and even more often than meat, chicken is served. It is probably to be lamb if the meat is included in a dish. Sometimes roasted or marinated, meats and veggies produce extremely robust and velvety tastes. Lime, olive oil, and cloves are three ingredients that appear in nearly any Lebanese bowl. Garlic is commonly fried in food, and olive oil is frequently used to cover dishes, where its fragile taste comes alive. Lime is used liberally in authentic Lebanese cuisine, particularly salads. For more spice and improved results, the Lebanese also fry with a nut-based fat, like peanut oil. A direct expression of its accommodating community is the Lebanese food.

Lebanon's food is the culmination of the Mediterranean lifestyle. This involves an excess of starches, citrus, plants, fresh seafood; wisely eating animal fats. Food is most commonly either fried, grilled, or steamed in olive oil; other than a few sweets, milk, or cream is scarcely used. Sometimes raw or marinated as well as fried, veggies are consumed. Although Lebanon's food does not have a whole sauce range, it relies on spices, herbs, and product freshness; there are almost no limitations to the range of meals and variations. The foods are full of hearty, aromatic flavors, and much of what the Lebanese consume is determined by the weather, as it is in most Mediterranean areas.

The Ottomans, which ruled Lebanon for more than four centuries, had the greatest influence on Lebanese food. Lamb had become the preferred meat under Ottoman rule, and vegetables and fruit stuffing became common and solid deep Ground coffee. The Ottomans are also responsible for the Lebanese's tasty baklava and many almonds, vegetables, and baked goods.

Once the Ottomans were destroyed in WW1, the French invaded Lebanon and brought a very new ethnic cuisine. Although the French were only here till 1946, they undoubtedly had a lasting effect.

The French had the greatest impact on the entire cuisine through their desserts and sweets, including croissants and caramel flan, which are still popular today. Lebanon has established ties with other regions of the world for a long time, which is why you will find ingredients that come from all corners of the globe in their cuisine. Beirut, Lebanon's city, was once recognized as the "Middle East Paris," with nomadic tribes traveling by all manner of exotic delights to the Far East, like fresh fruits and seasoning. Today, in almost every nation on earth, Lebanese people live and always bring fresh spices, tastes, and cultures back to Lebanon when they return home for holidays.

Beverages are very occasionally served in Lebanon without it being supplemented by food. The style or tradition in which their cuisine is often eaten is one of the healthier and most exciting elements of Lebanese cuisine, refers to as mezze. While basic fresh fruits are often eaten at the end of a Lebanese dinner, desserts and coffee are also present. A famous Lebanese dessert, Baklava, generally associated with Greek food, is also common. In Lebanon, coffee is a massive priority. It is consumed during the day, in public markets, and at homes. Lebanese coffee is solid, smooth, and sometimes cardamom-flavored. It is typically heavily sweetened as well. The Mediterranean area's cuisine is a joyous occasion; it is fresh, tasty, vibrant, and energizing.

Lebanese diet depends heavily on olive oil, which could do miracles to reduce cholesterol, regulate blood glucose levels and improve optimal heart health, rather than baking with butter, cheese, or other milk products. In comparison to other Western cultural foods, Lebanese cuisine includes relatively few starchy products.

A small portion of grain or lentils is more likely to be seen than a massive serving of potatoes, pasta, or heavily refined white bread. The meat of preference in Lebanon was always sheep, which is viewed as a much healthier alternative than saturated fat. Grass-fed lamb and a perfect origin of fatty acids are rich in protein, niacin, magnesium, B12 vitamin, zinc, and phosphate.

Mint used in Lebanese food refreshes the breath, improves metabolism, and has been discovered to benefit everything from losing weight to migraine prevention. However, parsley is rich in vitamins C, K, and A and folate, iron, and zinc. "Lebanese Cookbook" has a wide range of Lebanese recipes with different ingredients and methods. It has three chapters based on Breakfast, snack, lunch, dinner, salad, soups, and sides' recipes. All recipes with lots of health benefits are here. Try these recipes and make your meal more delightful and flavorful.

Chapter 1: Lebanese Breakfast Recipes

1.1 Manakish

Cooking Time: 2 hours 12 minutes
Serving Size: 6

Ingredients:
Dough Ingredients

- 1½ teaspoon active dry yeast
- 3 cups bread flour
- 1 tablespoon white granulated sugar
- 1 cup warm water
- 1 teaspoon salt
- ⅓ cup vegetable oil

Cheese Toppings

- 1 cup akawi cheese
- 1 cup mozzarella cheese
- 6 tablespoon olive oil
- 6 tablespoon za'atar

Method:

1. In a large mixing cup, add sugar, ½ cup of water, and yeast. Set it aside for fifteen minutes.
2. Add flour and remaining water and mix the dough in a food processor.
3. Gradually add the oil and mix at high speed until the dough is formed.
4. Cover the dough with a kitchen towel and let it rise for 40-45 minutes.
5. Put akawi cheese in cold water for 10 minutes.
6. Combine the mozzarella and akawi cheese together.
7. Heat up the oven to 425 degrees.
8. Divide dough into six flatbreads and add toppings.
9. Bake for 10 to 15 minutes until nicely browned.
10. Serve warm or store in the refrigerator.

1.2 Knafeh

Cooking Time: 40 minutes
Serving Size: 8

Ingredients:
- ½ cup ricotta cheese
- Crushed pistachios
- ½ phyllo dough 16-ounce box
- 2 cups mozzarella cheese
- ½ cup unsalted butter

For Knafeh Filling
- 3 tablespoons cream of wheat
- 3 tablespoons sugar
- 3 cups whole milk

For Rose Water Syrup
- 1 tablespoon lemon juice
- 1 teaspoon rose water
- ¾ cup water
- 1 cup granulated sugar

Method:
Rose Water Syrup
1. Combine water and sugar in a pan and boil.
2. Add lemon juice and simmer for 15 minutes.
3. Turn off the heat and add rose water.
4. Quickly stir and set it aside to cool completely.

Dough
1. Knead the phyllo dough and cut it into tiny pieces.
2. Add the small pieces into melted butter and mix until well coated with butter.
3. Set it aside.

Knafeh Fillings
1. Mix all the filling ingredients on low heat and boil.
2. Simmer for 5 minutes when the mixture starts to thicken.

3. Remove from heat and set aside.

Baking
1. Heat the oven to 370 degrees.
2. Oil the baking tray and spread the phyllo dough.
3. Add the shredded cheese and fillings.
4. Bake for thirty minutes.
5. Pour over some sugar syrup and serve with nuts toppings.

1.3 Quince Jam

Cooking Time: 90 minutes
Serving Size: 5 jars

Ingredients:
- 1 tablespoon lemon zest
- 4 cups sugar
- 4 ¼ cups water
- ¼ cup lemon juice
- 6 cups (packed) of quince

Method:
1. Wash and grate the quince.
2. Add water into a bowl and bring to boil.
3. Add lemon zest, quince, and lemon juice. Simmer for 10 minutes.
4. Add sugar and mix until well combined.
5. Bring to boil and lower the heat until the mixture starts to thicken.
6. Turn the heat off when the jam reaches its desired consistency.
7. Pour into jars and close the lid tightly.

1.4 Smoked Salmon Puffs

Cooking Time: 30 minutes
Serving Size: 8

Ingredients:

- 3.5 oz. goat cheese
- 1 tablespoon caper in brine
- 14 oz. puff pastry sheet
- 7 oz. smoked salmon

Method:
1. Put the puff pastry sheet in the fridge overnight.
2. Heat the oven to 400 degrees.
3. Add the smoked salmon onto the puff pastry sheet.
4. Cut into pizza shapes.
5. Bake the pastry in the oven until nicely browned.
6. Top with caper and cheese. Serve warm or keep in the refrigerator.

1.5 Crustless Tuna Quiche

Cooking Time: 25 minutes
Serving Size: 4

Ingredients:
- ½ teaspoon salt or to taste
- A dash of black pepper
- 1 onion, finely chopped
- 2 tablespoons canola oil
- 6 eggs
- ½ cup Swiss cheese, grated
- 2 cans of water-packed tuna
- 1/3 cup heavy cream
- 1 cup milk

Method:
1. Heat the oven to 400 degrees.
2. Spray muffin cups with oil.
3. Sauté the onion for five minutes until translucent.
4. In a bowl, mix the remaining ingredients.
5. Add onion to the bowl mixture.
6. Mix and pour into muffin cups.

7. Bake for twenty minutes until the surface color starts to change.

1.6 Shakshuka

Cooking Time: 30 minutes
Serving Size: 6
Ingredients:
- ¼ cup parsley leaves
- ¼ cup mint leaves
- ½ cup tomato sauce
- 6 large eggs
- Extra-virgin olive oil
- Salt and pepper
- 6 Vine-ripe tomatoes
- 1 large yellow onion, chopped
- ½ teaspoon ground cumin
- Pinch red pepper flakes
- 2 green peppers, chopped
- 1 teaspoon ground coriander
- 1 teaspoon sweet paprika
- 2 garlic cloves, chopped

Method:
1. Take a pan and heat olive oil.
2. Add vegetables except for tomato. Add spices and mix.
3. Turn the heat down and simmer for 5 minutes.
4. Add the tomatoes and tomato sauce and cook for 15 minutes until it thickens.
5. Make 6 holes into the mixture and add eggs in each hole.
6. Wait until egg whites are cooked.
7. Remove from heat, add garnish and serve hot.

1.7 Lebanese Eggs with Lamb and Pine Nuts

Cooking Time: 20 minutes
Serving Size: 4

Ingredients:
- 2 tablespoon toasted pine nuts
- 1 tablespoon chopped green scallion
- 4 eggs, beaten
- Salt to taste
- 1 tablespoon olive oil
- 1 clove garlic, crushed
- 1 teaspoon seven spices seasoning
- ¼ lb. ground lamb
- ¼ cup onion, chopped

Method:
1. Heat a pan and add olive oil.
2. Add onion and sauté for 5 minutes.
3. Insert lamb, garlic, and spices. Mix and cook until nicely browned.
4. Add eggs and bake for ten minutes in the oven at 400 degrees temperature.
5. Top with nuts and scallions.

1.8 Easy Lebanese Fatteh with chickpeas

Cooking Time: 15 minutes
Serving Size: 4

Ingredients:
- 3 tablespoon butter
- 1 teaspoon salt divided
- 2 tablespoon tahini
- Handful pine nuts
- 4-5 pitta bread squares
- Vegetable oil for frying
- Juice of ½ lemon

- 1-2 garlic cloves
- 3 cups yogurt unsweetened
- 1 can chickpeas with water

Method:
1. Fry the bread squares and put them on kitchen towels.
2. Prepare pine nuts and set them aside.
3. In a pan, add chickpeas and boil. Add salt and lemon juice.
4. Grate the garlic in a large mixing bowl.
5. Add tahini, yogurt, and ½ teaspoon salt.
6. Heat butter until brown and set it aside.
7. Dip the bread into chickpea water and remove it immediately.
8. Put in a plate and add chickpea and water.
9. Add tahini mixture and drizzle with some nuts on top.
10. Add lemon and salt. Serve immediately.

1.9 Fatteh with Hummus

Cooking Time: 30 minutes
Serving Size: 6

Ingredients:
- 1 pinch paprika
- 3 to 4 mint leaves
- ½ cup olive oil
- 2 tablespoons pine nuts
- 2 cups chickpeas, dry
- 1 pinch salt
- 5 small pita loaves
- 3 cups natural yogurt
- 1 pinch cumin
- 1 pinch white pepper (optional)
- ½ lemon, juiced
- 2 garlic cloves, crushed

- 2 tablespoons tahini

Method:
1. Soak chickpeas in water overnight and bring to boil with some salt.
2. Simmer for 1 hour until soft.
3. Add yogurt, garlic, salt, and tahini to a bowl.
4. Bring some water to boil. Indirect heat yogurt placing the bowl on boiling water pan.
5. Add spices to the sauce.
6. Fry bread and cut it into small pieces.
7. On a large plate, add the bread and pour chickpea broth.
8. Add a second layer of bread and add chickpea broth.
9. Mix gently with a spatula and add yogurt mixture.
10. Toast pine nuts and add them to the plate.
11. Insert paprika, mint leaves, and pepper on top. Serve immediately.

1.10 Eggs and Meat

Cooking Time: 7 minutes
Serving Size: 4

Ingredients:
- A dash of allspice
- A dash of black pepper
- 1 tablespoon butter
- 2 tablespoons canola oil
- 250g ground lamb
- ½ teaspoon salt or to taste
- 6 eggs

Method:
1. Insert the ground meat into a large pan and cook for around five minutes over medium-high heat, just until the fluids are removed.

2. To the ground beef, add the oil and the butter and sprinkle with salt and seasoning.
3. Create six holes in the golden-brown beef pan using the front of a large spoon and then add them.
4. Place a cover under the pan and cook for ten minutes over medium heat until the whites are firm and the yolk is mildly watery or based on your preference.

1.11 Ful Medames

Cooking Time: 30 minutes
Serving Size: 4

Ingredients:
- 1 teaspoon cumin
- ½ teaspoon kosher salt
- 1, 15 ounces can chickpeas
- 2, 14 ounces can fava beans

Sauce for Topping
- 1 tablespoon chopped jalapenos
- Salt and pepper to taste
- ½ cup extra virgin olive oil
- ½ cup chopped parsley
- 4 garlic cloves crushed
- ¼ cup lemon juice

Method:
1. To wash, spill the fava beans as well as the chickpeas all together in a saucepan.
2. In ice water, wash the beans.
3. Convert, over a moderate flame, the washed, soaked beans to a small saucepan and insert two and a half cups of ice water. Use cumin and sea salt to sprinkle.
4. Carry it to a boil with the combination.

5. Turn off the heat and let stirring occasionally revealed for 20 minutes after most of the liquid is consumed, trying to smash to have the right consistency now and then with the edge of a spoon.
6. In the meantime, mix in a shallow saucepan all the food items for the sauce.
7. Offer the mixture on top and next to the Ful Medames whenever the beans and chickpeas are finished cooking.
8. With the bean combination, you can mix half of the seasoning and represent the other half on one side.
9. Offer together with hot pita, radishes, and tomatoes with chopped basil on edge.

1.12 Lebanese Omelette with Almond Hummus

Cooking Time: 15 minutes
Serving Size: 2
Ingredients:
- 1 tablespoon Za'atar
- 1 bunch parsley
- 4 tablespoons lemon juice
- 4 eggs
- 2 teaspoons ground cumin
- 200g (7oz.) almond meal

Method:
1. Put the almond meal, 7oz. of liquid, cumin, lime juice, and just a little spice in a large jug or container for the almond hummus.
2. Purée to produce a deep, smooth paste using our food processor. With more salts and lime, spray.
3. For za'atar oil, mix za'atar in a shallow container or cup with two tablespoons of olive oil and a bit of salt.

4. For an omelet, add two eggs with a pinch of salt and two teaspoons of water in a shallow cup.
5. On a moderate flame, warm a small deep fryer.
6. Insert a drizzle of olive oil once the pan is hot, and then move to cover the pan's bottom.
7. Insert the eggs and simmer softly until they are no longer watery.
8. Turn the heat off if they appear to sizzle quickly. You need to prepare the eggs carefully so that they do not overcook.
9. Push the omelet into a tray once the eggs are finished.
10. Repeat to produce a new omelet with the leftover eggs.
11. Spoon nut hummus over the edge of the omelets to prepare.
12. Spread on one side of the rosemary/lettuce/tabouleh. Rain flavored oil over it.

1.13 Baked Eggs with Sumac, Spinach & Spring Onions

Cooking Time: 50 minutes
Serving Size: 4

Ingredients:
- Hot buttered toast, to serve
- Chilli sauce, to serve
- 8 medium eggs
- Salt and ground black pepper
- 2 teaspoon olive oil
- ½ teaspoon sumac, plus extra to serve
- 200g baby spinach leaves
- 4 spring onions, roughly chopped
- 1 teaspoon ground coriander
- A pinch of dried chili flakes
- 1 garlic clove, sliced

Method:

1. Preheat the oven to 200°C.
2. In a wide skillet, add the oil and insert the green onions, garlic, cilantro, chili, sumac, and lettuce.
3. Bring a good swirl to all and enable the spinach to wilt in the flame of the pot.
4. Switch the leaves over so they are beneath the ones that have not begun cooking.
5. Split it up approximately into quarters, then place each portion in a container or dish that is deep, ovenproof.
6. Force it along the sides of the cups so the eggs have room in the center. Crush each bowl with two eggs.
7. Wrap in foil and cook for twenty minutes or until the eggs are set.
8. Offer the spicy bread and the hot sauce, filled with sumac.

1.14 Foul – Lebanese Vegan Fava Bean Breakfast

Cooking Time: 25 minutes
Serving Size: 6

Ingredients:

- 1 tomato
- Olive oil for serving
- 1 teaspoon salt
- ½ bunch parsley
- 2 tablespoon tahini paste
- 1 teaspoon ground cumin
- 3 14-oz. canned cooked fava beans
- 5 cloves garlic
- 1 lemon juiced
- 1 15.5oz chickpeas canned

Method:

1. Transfer to a big pot the fava beans and their water.
2. The chickpeas are drained and rinsed and added to the bowl of fava beans.
3. With a tablespoon of salt, smash the cloves. Add juice from a lemon.
4. To a serving dish, transfer the heated fava bean and chickpea combination.
5. Crush the ginger, smash the beans and chickpeas with the fava.
6. Insert finely chopped garlic, lime juice, cilantro, and spice, and tahini sauce.
7. Blend and mix.
8. For a kick, add half a teaspoon of chili powder or other spicy pepper.
9. Thinly slice the parsley and tomato leaf and set it aside to serve.
10. Offer with a mixture of sliced parsley and onions and rain with some olive oil.

1.15 Za'atar Omelets with Olives, Feta and Leftover Toast

Cooking Time: 10 minutes
Serving Size: 2

Ingredients:

- Salt and pepper
- 1 tablespoon olive oil
- 5 olives (pitted)
- 1 slice of leftover bread
- 1 tablespoon feta
- 2 eggs
- 1 tablespoon za'atar

Method:

1. In a cup, combine the eggs and sprinkle them with salt.

2. On a moderate fire, put a non-stick bowl.
3. Transfer the olive oil to a pan and split the toast and olives into bits.
4. To the bowl, add it.
5. Beat the eggs to the bowl, insert the za'atar, and then the feta.
6. Cover the pan and steam until the whole omelet is finished.

Chapter 2: Lebanese Snack Recipes

2.1 Spanish Orange and Almond Cake

Cooking Time: 1 hour
Serving Size: 6

Ingredients:
- 1 tablespoon water
- 1 teaspoon sugar vanilla
- 200g white sugar
- 225g ground almond
- 100g butter, softened
- 1/3 cup of coconut oil
- 5 eggs, separated
- 2 whole oranges

For the Orange Chips
- 1/3 cup icing sugar
- 1 medium-sized orange
- ½ cup sugar
- 1/3 cup slivered almonds

Method:
1. Heat the stove to 350°F. In the middle of the oven, put a tray.
2. Wipe and rub the oranges to dry. Chop into tiny cubes.
3. In a frying pan, put the orange squares and a pint of water over medium heat.
4. Heat and cook for thirty minutes. Set that aside and let it cool completely.
5. Put the oranges that have been cooked in a mixing bowl. Just set aside.
6. Beat the eggs, put only half a cup of sugar, and continue to beat till soft peaks are formed.
7. Add the butter, remaining sweetener, vanilla sugar, and egg whites to a large bowl.

8. Beat this for two minutes.
9. Add the ground nuts and stir in the oranges that are finely sliced.
10. Ladle the batter into the baking dish for fifty minutes just until the middle of the cake has a skewer inserted, and it tends to come out dry. Put down to refrigerate.
11. Heat the stove to 200°F.
12. In the middle of the oven, put a shelf.
13. Spray ¼ cup artificial sweeteners with an oven dish.
14. Put the glucose with the orange pieces and toss the remainder of the sugar with the pieces.
15. On the stove, toast the orange pieces and check them after fifteen minutes.
16. Take the dish out of the oven and then let the orange chips cool completely. Spray the cake on edge.

2.2 Cheese and Pastirma Turnovers

Cooking Time: 55 minutes
Serving Size: 40 pieces
Ingredients:
- 1 egg
- 200g pastirma, cut into strips
- 200g goat feta cheese
- 400g Emmental cheese
- 5 sheets of rolled puff pastry

For the Egg Wash
- 1 egg, lightly beaten

Method:
1. Heat up the oven to 400° F. In the middle of the oven, put a shelf.
2. Mix the Cheese, crushed feta, pastirma, and omelet strips in a tray. Mix well to combine fully.

3. A worktop will lightly flour and cut it up one puff bread sheet at the moment.
4. Get the other wraps refrigerated.
5. Split the puff pastry layer into eight equivalent squares and use a pizza cutter.
6. Put a heapy filling spoonful in the middle of each block.
7. Slide it into a triangle across each block.
8. To crimp the sides, just use the tines of a spoon.
9. Move the turnovers onto a baking sheet filled with parchment.
10. Refrigerate for approximately 20 minutes.
11. Use the egg wash to scrub each turnover.
12. Cook for 20-25 minutes or until the shade is translucent.

2.3 Zalabia (Lebanese Sweet Fritters)

Cooking Time: 30 minutes
Serving Size: 4
Ingredients:
- 1½ tablespoon active dry yeast
- 3 cups canola oil
- 1 tablespoon powdered milk
- ¾ or 1 cup lukewarm water
- 2 tablespoons white sesame seeds
- 2 tablespoons whole anise seeds
- 2½ cups all-purpose flour
- 3 tablespoons sugar
- ¼ cup canola oil

Method:
1. Mix the flour, dried yeast, sugar, pumpkin seeds, anise seeds, dairy, and oil in a container.
2. Add warm water. With the middle of your hands, blend and whisk rigorously.
3. Protect and set it aside for one hour with a smooth dishtowel.

4. Nearly the size of an omelet cut the mixture into equitable balls.
5. Use the finger of your hands to push each ball into a snack texture.
6. Gently deflate each roll and use a spoon.
7. Penetrate with your finger to create three holes for each dough.
8. Add the oil to a higher temperature sufficient and roast the dough in samples to a golden color.
9. Erase on paper towels with a serving dish and drain.

2.4 Lebanese Sandwich

Cooking Time: 35 minutes
Serving Size: 2

Ingredients:
- Chile flakes, to taste
- Sprinkle of olive oil
- ¼ cup of pitted olives
- 20 fresh mint leaves
- 2 slices of onion
- 1 shredded lettuce leaf
- 2 pita bread
- 3 tablespoon za'atar
- 1 tomato, sliced
- 2 tablespoon olive oil

Method:
1. The oven must be preheated to 500 °F.
2. Put the bread on the baking tray.
3. Combine the oil and the za'atar in a shallow saucepan.
4. On the pastry, stretch the combination.
5. Cook it for two minutes in the oven.
6. Put on the bread with the rest of the ingredients and squirt with coconut oil.
7. Roll the pastry and instantly serve.

2.5 Lebanese Halloumi and Eggs Recipe

Cooking Time: 10 minutes
Serving Size: 2

Ingredients:
- Paprika
- Olive oil for shallow frying
- Two tablespoons Greek yogurt
- Freshly chopped mint
- 4 eggs
- 4 slices halloumi cheese

Method:
1. In a non-stick deep fryer, steam a large slick of coconut oil.
2. To the plate, transfer the halloumi and shade it on the one hand.
3. In order to keep the cheese located underneath the egg, beat the eggs on the halloumi.
4. Roast the eggs till the yolk is already watery and the surface has dried.
5. On a pan, spray with paprika and top.
6. In order to produce a gloopy dressing, blend the yogurt with fresh basil and ample water.
7. Sprinkle over the eggs with the seasoning and serve warm.

2.6 Lebanese Hash

Cooking Time: 40 minutes
Serving Size: 4

Ingredients:
- 1 tomato, chopped
- 1 bunch spinach, chopped
- ½ teaspoon ground allspice
- 1 teaspoon water
- 2 tablespoons olive oil

- Salt and pepper
- 6 eggs
- 1 red bell pepper, chopped
- 1 zucchini, chopped
- 1 onion, chopped
- ½ eggplant, peeled
- 8 mushrooms, chopped
- 1 potato, peeled

Method:
1. Melt the butter over medium-high heat in a really large skillet.
2. Add the onions and continue cooking for a couple of minutes.
3. Insert the potato and proceed to simmer for a few minutes, stirring regularly.
4. Sprinkle with seasonings the potato, eggplant, and onion combination.
5. Add the onions, peppers, and sweet potato, mixing after each inclusion and adding a little more salt and black pepper, one component at a time.
6. Increase the power down just a bit and mix the allspice, eggs, and water.
7. Transfer to the mixture and add until the eggs with the veggies are scrambled.
8. Insert the tomatoes and the basil when the eggs are mostly done and mix only enough to lose steam the spinach.
9. Serve with milk, pieces of radish, cucumbers, fresh basil, and rye bread instantly.
10. Break off little bits of the flatbread to consume and use them to scrape up the hash.

2.7 Lebanese Msabaha

Cooking Time: 10 minutes
Serving Size: 4

Ingredients:
For the Hummus

- Pepper
- Some parsley
- 4 tablespoon olive oil
- Salt
- 1 can chickpeas
- 4 tablespoon lemon juice
- 2-3 tablespoon Tahini
- 2 cloves garlic

For the Side Dish

- ½ bunch fresh parsley
- 4-5 flatbreads
- 1 handful olives
- ½ bunch fresh mint
- 1 red onion
- ½ cucumber
- 2 tomatoes
- 1 cup vegan yogurt

Method:
1. Wash the chickpeas in a pan and gather the juice.
2. Purée three-quarters of the chickpeas in a processor along with two teaspoons of lime juice, some Tahini, Aqua Farber, and two tiny cloves of garlic.
3. Blend to the finest degree imaginable.
4. With salt and black pepper, prepare the hummus and put it in a dish.
5. Create a depression in the core of the hummus.
6. Combine the leftover vegetable oil and lime juice with pepper and salt, season.

7. Place the hummus along with the chickpeas. If you like, add additional olive oil with it.
8. Slice the spring onions into circles and the cucumber and vegetables into pieces for the side salad. Drain any olives.
9. Slice some of the clean rosemary and fresh mint and cut the remainder thinly.
10. Seasoning the yogurt with pepper and mix in the rosemary and basil.
11. Use the cucumber, cabbage, tomato, onions, dried basil, yogurt, and naan bread to eat the Msabaha.

2.8 Kaak (Lebanese Street Bread)

Cooking Time: 27 minutes
Serving Size: 4
Ingredients:
- Milk for brushing
- Sesame seeds about two tablespoon
- Warm water
- Olive oil one tablespoon
- All-purpose flour one ¾ cup
- Salt 1 teaspoon
- Warm milk ¾ cup
- Whole wheat flour ½ cup
- Sugar 2 tablespoon
- Active dry yeast ½ tablespoon

Method:
1. Insert the yeast, sugar, and milk and combine properly.
2. Roll it up for ten minutes and then let it grow.
3. Transfer the rice, salts, oil, and fermentation solution to the mixer cup.
4. Start combining the flour once they come around, using a flour hook.

5. For around seven to eight minutes, make the dough and then put it in a lubricated bowl to soar.
6. Fill a bowl and then let the dough rise before the amount doubles.
7. Break it into four balls of the same dimension.
8. Create two baking sheets that are lined with paper towels.
9. Print out a circle from the narrow portion of the wrapped dough using a cookie cutter.
10. Protect the containers and leave to proof the rounded bread for approximately thirty minutes or until mildly puffy.
11. Heat a 425 F microwave.
12. Brush it with a beaten egg until the bread has stopped rising.
13. Spray the seeds with sesame.
14. Cook until golden, then eat after 10 minutes.

2.9 Cheese Manakish

Cooking Time: 17 minutes
Serving Size: 1
Ingredients:
- 4 tablespoon regular olive oil
- ¼ cup vegetable oil
- 1 teaspoon of salt
- ½ teaspoon of sugar
- 500 g Akkawi cheese
- 1 cup of lukewarm water
- 1 tablespoon of dried active yeast
- 3 ¼ cups of plain or bread flour

Method:
1. Get the Akkawi cheese prepared.

2. Add the sugar and the drained effective fermentation to the luke-warm water and mix until it disperses.
3. Let the yeast burst for fifteen minutes.
4. Place the salts and starch, the butter, and the yeast fluid in a big bowl and combine until you have a thick ball.
5. Make the dough for around ten minutes when you're using a hand blender.
6. Let it grow for at least two hours or until the scale has doubled.
7. Heat a big, hot, nonstick pan on the burner. On medium heat, put your broiler.
8. Pull out a tiny handful of around 3-5millimeters wide dough and pass it to the frying skillet.
9. Rub on a reasonable amount of olive oil and apply a decent amount of cheese and leave a small gap by rubbing it with your fingertips.
10. Fully dimple the layer a few moments with right hand upraised.
11. Switch the plate to the grill and bake from the above until crispy for the next five minutes after the top of the Manakish cheese has fried.

2.10 Hummus with Tahini

Cooking Time: 20 minutes
Serving Size: 6
Ingredients:
- Paprika for serving
- Fresh parsley for serving
- ½ teaspoon salt
- Extra-virgin olive oil
- 15 ounce can chickpeas beans
- 2 tablespoons tahini
- 2 garlic cloves
- 3 tablespoons lemon juice

Method:

1. In a bowl of hot water, put the chickpeas and scrub them together just to scrape off the skin.
2. Wash and move the garbanzo bean to a mixing bowl.
3. Mix them separately, scratching down the sides as required, until they are flour.
4. Apply the lime juice, tahini, spice, and garlic, and two ice cubes and mix until creamy for around five minutes.
5. By inserting more lime juice or spice, taste, and change as required.
6. Ladle the hummus onto a sheet or cup, then scatter the hummus to make flecks with the sides of the pan.
7. Sprinkle with canola oil, brush with chopped basil, and paprika.
8. Offer at ambient temperature or freezing.

Chapter 3: Lebanese Lunch Recipes

3.1 Homemade Beef Shawarma

Cooking Time: 30 minutes
Serving Size: 4

Ingredients:

- 1 ½ teaspoon salt
- ½ teaspoon black pepper
- 2 tablespoon distilled white vinegar
- 2 teaspoon shawarma spice
- 2 tablespoon vegetable oil
- 1 lb. sliced beef rib eye

Shawarma Spice Mix

- 0.25 teaspoon turmeric
- 0.25 teaspoon ground ginger
- ½ teaspoon ground cinnamon
- 0.25 teaspoon ground coriander
- 1 teaspoon cumin
- 1 teaspoon all-spice

Method:

1. Start by cutting into 3-inch thinly sliced of your meat.
2. Merge the olive oil with the white vinegar to start making the marinade.
3. Add the flavor, black pepper, to the Shawarma.
4. Blend them with the beef rigorously and cover them with cling film and return to the refrigerator.
5. Sauté the meat for fifteen minutes in a skillet over medium-high heat, after most flavorings have faded away.
6. For the sandwich or tortilla, chop all of your veggies.
7. Start opening a pita to make your burger and assemble the meat and all of your fixings.

8. Sprinkle on top with the Tahini sauce.

3.2 Easy Homemade Pita Chips Recipe

Cooking Time: 22 minutes
Serving Size: 8
Ingredients:
- 1 teaspoon salt
- ½ teaspoon pepper
- 2 tablespoons olive oil
- 3 tablespoons za'atar
- 4 pieces large pita bread white

Method:
1. Heat the oven to 350 degrees and line the foil with two cooking layers.
2. Sprinkle with spray for cooking and set it aside.
3. Chop the flatbread in the quarter and then in the quarter again, and use a pair of scissors.
4. Till you have chip-sized bits, proceed with doing this.
5. In a large mixing bowl, put the pita squares, drizzle them with olive oil, and then toss them with za'atar, black pepper, and salt.
6. Mix well until the pita is equitably coated with seasonings and oil.
7. Spread the pita between both cookie sheets in an even coating and bake for about ten minutes until shining nicely browned.
8. Mix thoroughly or store for up to five days in a sealed jar.

3.3 Quick-Roasted Tomatoes with Thyme and Garlic

Cooking Time: 30 minutes
Serving Size: 6

Ingredients:

- Extra virgin olive oil
- Crumbled feta cheese
- 1 teaspoon sumac
- ½ teaspoon dry chili pepper flakes
- 2 lb. smaller tomatoes, halved
- Kosher salt and black pepper
- 2 teaspoon fresh thyme
- 2 to 3 garlic cloves, minced

Method:

1. Heat the oven to 450°F.
2. In a mixing bowl, put the tomato slices.
3. Add the chopped garlic, salt, paprika, seasonings, and fresh herbs.
4. Drizzle with a gracious amount of extra virgin olive, about ¼ cup or more. Toss to coat it.
5. Use a rim to transmit the vegetables to a baking tray.
6. Split the vegetables, flesh cut side, in one thin layer.
7. Roast for thirty minutes in your hot oven just until the vegetables have crumbled to your desired thickness.
8. Withdraw from the heat.
9. Try to flavor it with more grated parmesan and a few spritzes of cheddar cheese if you prepare to serve it quickly.

3.4 Mediterranean Chicken Kabobs

Cooking Time: 35 minutes
Serving Size: 4-6
Ingredients:
- 1 large red onion
- Vegetable oil
- 5 garlic cloves, minced
- 2- ½ pounds chicken thighs
- 1- ¾ teaspoons salt
- ½ teaspoon black pepper
- Zest from one lemon
- 2 tablespoons lemon juice
- 1 cup milk Greek yogurt
- ⅛ teaspoon cinnamon
- 1 teaspoon red pepper flakes
- 2 teaspoons paprika
- ½ teaspoon cumin
- 2 tablespoons olive oil

Method:
1. Mix the yogurt, vegetable oil, red pepper, smoked paprika, cardamom, and flakes of tarragon, lime juice, lemon zest, seasoning, pepper, and garlic in a small bowl.
2. Thread the poultry onto steel forks, pulling if the bits are stiff and lengthy, interchanging with the spring onions occasionally.
3. Be sure that the skewers are not crammed.
4. Put the kebabs on an aluminum foil-lined baking sheet.
5. Ladle the sauce or brush it all over the chicken, coating it well.
6. Cover and chill for a minimum of eight hours.
7. Heat the grill to a moderate flame.
8. Gently dip a bunch of paper towels in olive oil to lubricate the grill and cautiously rub over the

railings a few times, using tweezers, till shiny and covered.

9. Cook the chicken kebabs for five to ten minutes till lightly browned and grilled through, turning the forks frequently.

10.   Move and represent the skewers on a large plate.

3.5 Easy Hummus Recipe

Cooking Time: 1 hour 5 minutes
Serving Size: 4

Ingredients:

- ¼ teaspoon cumin
- 1 tablespoon cooking water
- ½ clove garlic
- The juice of the half lemon
- 1½ tablespoon extra-virgin olive oil
- ½ teaspoon salt
- 1 teaspoon baking soda
- 1½ tablespoon tahini
- 100 grams dried chickpeas

Method:

1. Moisten the chickpeas in ice water nightly.
2. At medium temperature, bring it to a boil and then stir until gentle on a low flame.
3. Flush the chickpeas but as you would want it, withhold a few of the liquid.
4. In the mixing bowl, place the chickpeas and mix for two minutes.
5. Add lime juice, tahini, extra virgin olive oil, and olive oil, and continue to mix until buttery.
6. Add the garlic, seasoning, and cilantro and mix until completely mixed and soft for four minutes.
7. If necessary, whisk the spices, trying to add more seasoning or lime.
8. Put one tablespoon of olive oil in a small bowl, rain, seasoning with a few chickpeas, and spritz with parmesan.
9. Store in refrigerator or serve immediately with chickpea seasoning.

3.6 Stuffed Grape Leaves (Dolmas)

Cooking Time: 2 hours 30 minutes
Serving Size: 60 grape leaves

Ingredients:
- 2 medium Yukon gold potatoes
- ¼ cup lemon juice
- ¼ teaspoon cinnamon
- 1 jar grape leaves
- 2 teaspoons 7 Spice
- 1 ½ cups short-grain white rice
- 2 tablespoons olive oil
- ½ teaspoon salt
- 1 pound ground beef

Method:
1. Sink and wash the grapevine leaf in a big bowl of hot water.
2. Split the leaves softly and wash them separately.
3. Heat the olive oil in a big skillet and cook the ground beef till it is golden brown.
4. Dress with seven spices and salt.
5. To the beef mince, substitute uncooked rice and seasoning and blended well once everything is integrated.
6. Place a grape leaf straight on a chopping board to fill and wrap the grape leaves.
7. Squeeze out the middle of the grape leaf with teaspoons of the rice combination.
8. Pull in the sides gently and roll it out like you would do when creating a wrap.
9. Place the potatoes or tomatoes at the bottom of a deep container and add salt and pepper.
10. Sprinkle with canola oil on each sheet and sprinkle with salt to compare.
11. To fully cover the grape leaves and pan, insert six cups of hot water.

12.   Cover the pot and continue cooking for thirty minutes after most of the water is consumed and the rice is prepared.
13.   On each of the grape leaves, pour the lime juice, then simmer on a moderate flame for an extra 45 minutes.
14.   Remove from the heat and then let chill for thirty minutes, exposed.
15.   Transfer to a bowl and serve!

3.7 Easy Falafel Recipe

Cooking Time: 30 minutes
Serving Size: 18

Ingredients:
- Oil for frying grapeseed
- Sesame seeds optional
- 1 teaspoon black pepper
- 1 teaspoon baking powder
- 1 pound dry chickpeas
- 2 teaspoons cumin
- 2 teaspoons coriander
- ¾ cup parsley
- 2 tablespoons flour
- 1 tablespoon salt
- ⅓ cup cilantro
- 1 garlic clove
- 1 small onion quartered

Method:
1. Wash the chickpeas in ice water nightly.
2. In the food processor, put the chickpeas and combine until they are flour.
3. Combine the tarragon, cilantro, cabbage, garlic, rice, cinnamon, cumin, coriander, and chili flakes with the mixture.
4. Cover and chill the container for 1 hour until set.

5. Spray baking soda on the falafel mixture when prepared to make, then gently press in.
6. With the falafel, form a circular shape, each with around 1-2 tablespoons of the combination.
7. In a deep fryer, deep-frying steam oil over moderate flame.
8. Place it softly in the deep fryer until it turns orange, around 2-3 minutes on either side.
9. With a serving dish, extract the falafel from the grease, and set it on a tray.

3.8 Layered Hummus Dip

Cooking Time: 10 minutes
Serving Size: 10

Ingredients:
- 1 tablespoon lemon juice
- Pita chips to serve
- 1 tablespoon olive oil
- 1 tablespoon za'atar
- 1 ten ounces Hummus
- 2 tablespoons
- 2 tablespoons pine nuts
- 1 Roma tomato
- ¼ cup scallions
- ½ cup cucumbers

Method:
1. Place hummus onto a serving platter or cooking platter in a small piece.
2. Spray the tomatoes, onions, green onions, parsley, cucumber, and pine nuts with the hummus.
3. Before eating with the pita chips, dust the dish with coconut oil, za'atar, and lime juice.

3.9 Easy Baba Ganoush Recipe

Cooking Time: 1 hour 5 minutes
Serving Size: 6

Ingredients:
- Olive oil
- Parsley
- 1 large eggplant
- 2 garlic cloves
- ¼ teaspoon salt
- 3-4 tablespoons lemon juice
- ¼ cup tahini

Method:
1. Preheat the oven to 400 degrees Fahrenheit.
2. Cover the eggplant in aluminum foil and bake until the eggplant is tender when stabbed with a spoon or fork.
3. Unscrew the eggplant and enable it ten minutes to settle.
4. Break off the surface and cut off the skin while the eggplant is cold to the touch.
5. Put the eggplant stuff in a mixing bowl or mixer.
6. Insert the lime slices, tahini, cloves of garlic, and salt.
7. Mix for two minutes until it is smooth and fluffy with the combination.
8. Garnish with coconut oil and tarragon.

3.10 Loaded Lebanese Rice

Cooking Time: 50 minutes
Serving Size: 6

Ingredients:
- ⅓ to ½ cup slivered almonds
- ½ cup dark raisins
- ½ cup fresh parsley leaves

- ⅓ to ½ cup pine nuts
- ¾ teaspoon ground cinnamon
- salt and pepper
- ½ teaspoon minced garlic
- ¾ teaspoon ground cloves
- 1 ½ cups medium-grain rice
- 1 lb lean ground beef
- 1 ¾ teaspoon ground allspice
- 1 small red onion
- Olive oil

Method:
1. For fifteen minutes, boil the rice in ice water.
2. In the meantime, in a large boiling kettle, heat the olive oil.
3. Add the sliced spring onions, cook them briefly over a moderate flame, then insert the minced beef.
4. Coat with allspice, garlic, spices, black pepper with the cooking liquid. Merge to toss.
5. Heat until you have thoroughly browned the beef.
6. Cover the rice with the beef.
7. Add a little salt to the rice and the rest of the pickles, ground cloves, and spices.
8. To coat the rice, add the water and vegetable oil.
9. Turn the heat down to medium, then cover; cook for twenty minutes.
10. Switch the pot's contents gently onto the large plate so that the beef layer now covers the rice.
11. Add parsley, buttered pine nuts, peanuts, and raisins to flavor.

3.11 Lebanese-Style Cinnamon Meatballs

Cooking Time: 50 minutes
Serving Size: 6

Ingredients:
For Meatballs

- ½ teaspoon red pepper
- Salt and pepper
- 1 teaspoon allspice
- ½ teaspoon cardamom
- ½ cup parsley
- 1 teaspoon cinnamon
- 1 slice sandwich bread
- ¾ cup yellow onions
- 2 to 3 garlic cloves
- 1 ½ lb. ground beef
- 1 egg
- ⅓ cup milk

For Sauce

- Salt and pepper
- Crushed red pepper flakes
- Extra virgin olive oil
- ½ teaspoon cinnamon
- ½ teaspoon allspice
- 1 tablespoon pomegranate molasses
- 2 bay leaves
- 1 cup grated yellow onion
- 2 garlic cloves
- 1 28-oz can tomatoes
- ½ cup water
- 1 carrot

Method:

1. Heat the oven to 375° F.
2. Put the toasted bread in a large pan and pour it with the liquid.

3. Let the loaf be soaked until very fluffy and soggy in the dairy.
4. Add the pizza, beef mince, and the leftover meatballs to a medium bowl.
5. Mix to blend, using washed palms.
6. Shape the combination of meat into meatballs. Bake for eleven to fifteen minutes or so in a hot oven at 375 degrees F.
7. Create the sauce whereas the meatballs are frying.
8. Heat up to 2 tablespoons of olive oil until it shimmers but does not flame.
9. Insert the onions and simmer for 5 minutes over a moderate flame, occasionally stirring, until translucent.
10. Insert the chopped garlic when tossing for a smooth thirty seconds.
11. Then add the onions, smashed tomatoes, and the supplies for the remaining sauce.
12. Take the liquid to a boil for around five minutes, then reduce the heat.
13. Transfer the meatballs to the liquid, cover, and boil until the meatballs are completely cooked across twenty minutes and more.
14. Garnish with clean grated parmesan.

3.12 Lebanese Chicken Fatteh Dinner Bowls

Cooking Time: 30 minutes
Serving Size: 6

Ingredients:
- Fresh parsley leaves
- 2 loaves Lebanese pita bread
- ½ cup toasted pine nuts
- 1 teaspoon sweet Spanish paprika
- 1 teaspoon ground sumac
- 1 medium yellow onion
- 3 garlic cloves, crushed

- ½ cup toasted sliced almonds
- 4 bone-in chicken breasts
- Water
- Extra virgin olive oil
- 4 whole cardamom pods
- 6 cloves
- Salt
- 2 dried bay leaves
- 2 cinnamon sticks
- 1 tablespoon apple cider vinegar

Mint Yogurt Sauce
- ½ cup chopped fresh mint
- Pinch salt
- 2 garlic cloves, crushed
- 1 ½ cup plain low-fat yogurt

Method:

1. In a small cup, put the yogurt, cloves, basil, and salt together.
2. Until well-combined, blend with a spoon.
3. In the meantime, cover and chill.
4. Organize the chicken breasts on the base of the large frying pan on a single sheet.
5. Spray salt on it.
6. Add the vinegar, basil leaves, cayenne pepper, cinnamon, and cloves to the apple cider.
7. Set the poultry pot over the moderate flame on the stove-top. Just get it to a boil.
8. Turn the heat down, cover it, and simmer for another twenty-minute.
9. Remove from the boiling broth with a rubber spatula and put it on a baking sheet to cool.
10. Under medium heat, heat two tablespoons olive oil.
11. Insert the vegetables and cook, constantly stirring, for four minutes.
12. Insert the cloves and simmer for about another second.

13.   Chicken, parmesan, and sumac are added. With salt and black pepper, spray.
14.   Mix until it is well-coated with the poultry.
15.   Heat until the chicken is fried completely, 5-7 minutes.
16.   Take and insert the toasted nuts. Seasoning with leaves of new parsley.

3.13 Homemade Labneh Recipe

Cooking Time: 24 hours
Serving Size: 8
Ingredients:
- ¾ teaspoon salt
- 32 oz. whole milk yogurt

Method:
1. Across a big jar, place the yogurt.
2. Mix the salt in. Line the huge bowl with a towel made of silk or muslin.
3. Place in the towel with the yogurt solution.
4. Pick up the sides of the towel and tie it at the end.
5. Hang up for 26 to 42 hours from a washer faucet to clean.
6. For stuffing, add hot pita and fresh vegetables.

3.14 Lebanese Rice with Vermicelli

Cooking Time: 35 minutes
Serving Size: 6
Ingredients:
- Salt
- ½ cup toasted pine nuts
- 1 cup broken vermicelli pasta
- 2 ½ tablespoon olive oil
- Water
- 2 cups long-grain rice

Method:
1. As per box directions, ready rice.
2. Melt the butter in a moderate, non-stick cooking pot.
3. Insert the vermicelli and constantly stir to toast it uniformly.
4. Transfer the rice and begin stirring so that the vegetable oil is well-coated with the rice. With pepper, season.
5. Now apply 3 ½ cups of water and put it to steam until the water decreases drastically.
6. Heat on medium for 15-20 minutes.
7. Switch to a baking tray and cover with the toasted cashews.

3.15 Kofta Kebab Recipe

Cooking Time: 20 minutes
Serving Size: 10
   Ingredients:
   - ½ teaspoon paprika
   - Pita bread to serve
   - ½ teaspoon ground sumac
   - ½ teaspoon ground nutmeg
   - ½ teaspoon cayenne pepper
   - ½ teaspoon ground green cardamom
   - Salt and pepper
   - 1 ½ teaspoon ground allspice
   - 1 medium yellow onion
   - ½ lb. ground lamb
   - 1 slice of bread
   - 2 garlic cloves
   - 1 lb. ground beef
   - 1 whole bunch of parsley

Method:

1. For around thirty minutes to 1 hour, soak ten wood skewers in liquid.
2. Slice the onions, cloves, and tarragon in a mixing bowl.
3. Insert the beef, lamb, bread, and seasoning.
4. Run the processors until it is all well mixed to create a mixture of pasty beef.
5. Take the stick blender from the braising liquid and put it in a wide tank.
6. Take a part of the meat mixture with a hand full and shape it on a wood skewer.
7. Till you have runs out of beef, repeat the procedure.
8. On a tray lined with paper towels laid the skewered kofta meatballs.
9. On the lightly floured, warmed gas grill, position the kofta meatballs.
10. Roast for four minutes on one surface on a moderate fire, switch over, and grill for another four minutes.
11. Get the kofta kebabs served.

Chapter 4: Lebanese Dinner Recipes

4.1 Lentils and Rice with Crispy Onions

Cooking Time: 1 hour 22 minutes
Serving Size: 4-6

Ingredients:
- Black pepper
- Parsley or parsley flakes
- 1 teaspoon kosher salt
- 1 cup long-grain white rice
- 1 cup black lentils
- ¼ cup extra virgin olive oil
- 2 large yellow onions
- 4 cups water

Method:
1. Layer the lentils and two cups of water in a shallow frying pan.
2. Under high heat, get the mixture to a boil.
3. Heat the oil over moderate heat in a large saucepan pan with a lid.
4. Insert the sliced onions and bake until the yellow onion is dark brown.
5. Measure the other 2 cups of water cautiously, bring the water to boiling over medium temperature, then reduce the heat to a simmer for two minutes.
6. Into the onion combination, whisk the rice and pre-cooked lentils.
7. Wrap and carry to a boil again. Turn off the heat and season with salt with black pepper.
8. With a rain of olive oil and tarragon garnish, eat the Mujadara warm or at ambient temperature.

4.2 Sumac Kebabs on Couscous Tabouli

Cooking Time: 1 hour
Serving Size: 4

Ingredients:

- Greek yogurt
- Pita bread
- 250g cherry tomatoes
- 60ml lemon juice
- 6 chicken thigh fillets
- 1 cup chopped flat-leaf parsley
- ½ cup chopped mint
- 2 cloves of crushed garlic
- 250 ml Massel chicken style liquid stock
- 190g couscous
- 1 tablespoon sumac
- 2 tablespoon virgin olive oil
- 1 teaspoon ground coriander

Method:

1. For fifteen minutes, soak twelve bamboo skewers in liquid.
2. Put the chicken, cloves, sumac, cilantro, and 1 tablespoon olive oil in a small dish.
3. With salt and black pepper, spice the blend and loop the poultry onto skewers.
4. Warm a char-grill plate or deep fryer over high heat.
5. Insert the chicken skewers, switch and turn until the chicken is crispy for 5-7 minutes.
6. Simmer the chicken broth in a large pan over medium temperature.
7. Remove from the heat afterward and insert couscous, and mix.
8. Put the couscous with the tarragon, basil, tomato, onions, lime juice, and remaining oil in a different dish. With salt and black pepper, spray.

9. Place the kebabs on the tops and serve them with flatbread and yogurt.

4.3 Slow-Cooker Persian lamb

Cooking Time: 40 minutes
Serving Size: 6 to 8

Ingredients:

- 1 dried lime
- 1 large pinch of saffron threads
- 1 cup dry white wine
- 1 cup fresh orange juice
- 1 lamb shoulder
- 1 head garlic
- 3 thyme sprigs
- Kosher salt and pepper
- 2 celery stalks
- 1 teaspoon dried dill
- 2 tablespoons olive oil
- 2 large carrots
- 2 large onions

Method:

1. Heat a slow cooker that is 5-to-6-quart.
2. Including salt and black pepper, spice the lamb.
3. Add the oil to a big, moderate Dutch oven.
4. Insert the lamb and cook for about ten minutes until lightly browned all over.
5. Switch to a slow cooker.
6. In the Dutch oven, add the onions, vegetables, fennel, and dill; roast, regularly mixing, until the vegetables are soft, five to six minutes.
7. Move the garlic, tarragon, vinegar, fruit juice, lemon, and saffron to the pressure cooker.
8. Heat and cook before meat falls apart and quickly shreds, seven to eight hours, on medium.
9. Skim out the ground fat. Offer over quinoa broth.

4.4 Roasted Beetroot Hummus with Dill and Yoghurt

Cooking Time: 10 minutes
Serving Size: 6

Ingredients:

- 2 heaping tablespoon tahini
- ¼ cup extra-virgin olive oil
- 1 small roasted beet
- 1 pinch salt and black pepper
- 2 large cloves of garlic
- 1 large lemon (zested)
- ½ large lemon
- 1 15-oz. can cooked chickpeas

Method:

1. Half beet and put it in your food processor until chilled and cleaned.
2. Blend until there are only little pieces left.
3. Insert the rest of the ingredients and combine until creamy, except for the olive oil.
4. Sprinkle in the olive oil while you blend the hummus.
5. When required, taste and change the spices, including more pepper, lime juice, or olive oil if necessary.
6. Add a little bit of liquid if that is too dense.
7. Keeps up to a week in the refrigerator.

4.5 Beef Kibbeh with Roasted Pumpkin Hummus

Cooking Time: 50 minutes
Serving Size: 4

Ingredients:
- 1 tablespoon olive oil
- 1 flax egg
- 1 cup pureed pumpkin
- All spices
- Sea salt and black pepper to taste
- 1¼ cup bulgur

For the Stuffing
- Pinch of nutmeg
- Canola oil or cooking spray
- 2 cloves of garlic
- 1 tablespoon of sumac
- 1 cup frozen spinach
- 1-2 tablespoon lemon juice
- 1 large onion
- 1 can of chickpeas
- 1 medium tomato
- ¼ cup toasted walnuts

Method:
1. Begin by steaming and pureeing the pumpkin in a mixing bowl and using a strong knife.
2. Heat the bulgur in the box and seasons, as guided.
3. In a large cup, add the pumpkin, spices, flax egg, bulgur, and vegetable oil and blend completely.
4. Pre-heat the furnace to 350 F.
5. Fry the vegetables and cloves in a saucepan over medium heat in some canola oil or olive oil and mist for 5-8 minutes once soft.

6. Transfer the diced tomatoes and the basil to compare and mix with the sumac, cinnamon, lime juice, salt, and black pepper.
7. Add some chickpeas.
8. Lubricate a moderate pan with some peanut oil spraying and start layering the pumpkin coating on the bowl's bottom.
9. On edge, scoop the filling.
10. Spray on top with some salt and black pepper and cook for 25-30 minutes or until mildly crispy at the edges.

4.6 Pea and Chickpea Falafel with Garlic Whipped Fetta

Cooking Time: 60 minutes
Serving Size: 6 to 8 falafel

Ingredients:
- 2 tablespoons flour
- Canola or vegetable oil
- ½ teaspoon black pepper
- 1 teaspoon baking soda
- ¼ teaspoon red pepper flakes
- 1 teaspoon salt
- 1 cup canned chickpeas
- ¼ cup fresh parsley leaves
- 1 ½ teaspoon ground cumin
- ¾ cup fresh peas
- 2 cloves garlic
- 1 tablespoon lemon juice
- ½ medium red onion

Method:
1. Transfer salted boiling hot water to a bowl of fresh peas and simmered for around five minutes, until soft.
2. Pour the water and fully chill the peas.

3. In a meal processor's tank, mix both components.
4. Change the seasoning as needed.
5. In a pan, heat approximately 1 inch of neutral oil on medium-high heat until it exceeds 350°F.
6. Shape the paste into tiny patties, respectively.
7. Start preparing and set aside a sheet pan lined with paper towels.
8. Before crowding the grill, cook the patties in clusters, a handful at a time.
9. Cook for about five minutes, stirring regularly, until glorious.
10. To cool, move to the lined baking sheet. Serve instantly.

4.7 Speedy Falafel and Black Rice Tabouli Bowl

Cooking Time: 40 minutes
Serving Size: 4
Ingredients:
- 3 tablespoon olive oil
- Sea salt, to taste
- Two teaspoons granulated garlic
- 2 teaspoon cumin
- 1 can chickpeas
- 1 handful parsley leaves
- ½ cup ground flaxseeds

Tabouli
- The drizzle of olive oil
- Sea salt, to taste
- ¼ white onion
- Handful mint
- Juice of ½ lime
- Handful cherry tomatoes
- Handful fresh basil
- 1 mini cucumber

Method:

1. Add all ingredients to a big bowl for the falafel, and blend until fully mixed.
2. Form with the palms into little balls, then bake for about thirty minutes in a 400F oven once crispy from the outside.
3. Transfer the sliced onions, cabbage, celery, and spices to a container for the tabouli.
4. Spray with just a little vegetable oil and lemon slices.
5. Salt and pour over the salad to taste.

4.8 Slow-Cooker Lebanese Freekeh

Cooking Time: 30 minutes
Serving Size: 4

Ingredients:

- ¼ teaspoon pepper
- ¼ cup minced fresh parsley
- 1 clove garlic grated
- ½ teaspoon salt
- 1 cup Cracked Freekeh
- 2 tablespoons tahini
- 2 tablespoons warm water
- 1 cup pomegranate seeds
- ½ cup blanched almond
- 1 juice of the lemon
- 15 ounce can chickpeas

Method:

1. As per product instructions, plan freekeh, then put in a wide cup.
2. Transfer the freekeh to the pan of sesame seeds and chickpeas.
3. Bake the almond pieces in a 350-degree oven for 5-7 minutes until golden brown, then return to the dish.

4. Mix all the tahini, lime juice, warm broth, garlic, salt, and black pepper in a small cup.
5. Rain over the chickpeas, freekeh, and pomegranate, then turn properly.
6. To eat, whisk in the toasted almonds and chopped parsley.

4.9 Lebanese-Style Lamb with Baby Potatoes and Honey Carrots

Cooking Time: 50 minutes
Serving Size: 4

Ingredients:
- 3 tablespoon white wine vinegar
- Honey
- 1 large sweet potato
- 2 carrots, peeled
- 8 lamb loin chops
- Kosher salt
- 1 teaspoon ground nutmeg
- 1 large red onion
- 1 Acorn Squash
- 2 teaspoon black pepper
- 1 ½ teaspoon paprika
- 1 head garlic
- 2 ½ teaspoon ground allspice
- ⅓ cup extra virgin olive oil

Method:
1. On both ends, season the lamb chops with sea salt.
2. Preheat the oven to 400°F. For two minutes, heat the acorn squash.
3. Break half of the acorn half lengthwise, then pick the seeds off.
4. Now, take every half of it and cut it into ½-inch thick circles.

5. Merge garlic powder, olive oil, one teaspoon of allspice, one teaspoon of smoked paprika, ¾ teaspoon of parmesan, and ½ teaspoon of ground cinnamon in a wide cup.
6. Mix thoroughly. With the garlic sauce, add the veggies to the broth dish.
7. With kosher salt, season. Insert the vinegar, red wine, and the leftover seasoning.
8. Mix thoroughly. Add in the lamb chops and flip to coat them.
9. Place to marinate. Place the veggies in a hot oven and bake for approximately 15 minutes.
10. After fifteen minutes, extract the veggies from the oven.
11. Place the sheep in the vegetable pan and place it back in the warm oven to bake for ten minutes.
12. Remove the pan from the heat when prepared, and instantly rain all the sheep and veggies with honey.

4.10 Beef and Hummus Wraps

Cooking Time: 15 minutes
Serving Size: 3

Ingredients:
- 1 baby cos lettuce
- ¼ cup Greek-style yogurt
- ½ cup hummus
- 2 large tomatoes
- Salt and black pepper
- 4 pieces mountain bread
- 2 tablespoon spice mix
- 800-gram sirloin steaks

Method:
1. Top the steaks with extra fat and dust with the Middle East spice blend.

2. On either side or once cooked as needed, cook sausages on a coated, oiled grill pan for about five minutes.
3. Use salt and black pepper to spray.
4. Serve the bread, hummus, onion, salad, and yogurt cut steaks.

4.11 Spiced Chermoula Lamb Rack with Quinoa Tabouli

Cooking Time: 40 minutes
Serving Size: 4

Ingredients:
- 1 tablespoons oil
- Crusty bread
- 2 tablespoons lemon juice
- 60g Persian Fetta
- 2/3 cup organic white grain quinoa
- 1½ cups flat-leaf parsley
- 200g Perino tomatoes
- 4 spring onions
- 1 cup mint leaves
- 1½ tablespoons olive oil
- 800g lamb rack roast
- 2 garlic cloves
- ½ teaspoon chili flakes
- 1 teaspoon paprika
- 1½ teaspoon cumin

Method:
1. Preheat the boiler to 190C.
2. Heat quinoa according to package instructions. Drain and thoroughly cool.
3. In the meantime, in a tiny jug, mix the chili, cumin, paprika, and one tablespoon of olive oil.

4. Place the lamb in a ceramic or wide glass bowl. Rub your marinade over your lamb. Place aside to marinate for thirty minutes.
5. On medium-high heat, heat the remaining olive oil in a large deep fryer.
6. Cook the lamb, rotating, for five minutes or until it's all golden brown.
7. For moderate or once cooked to your taste, put the lamb on a baking tray and roast for fifteen minutes.
8. Lamb's rest, protected for five minutes. Cut into chopped cutlets.
9. In a dish, mix the quinoa, parsley, spring onion, tomato, mint, ginger, and fetta oil.

4.12 Winter Chicken Tray Bake

Cooking Time: 2 hours 10 minutes
Serving Size: 6

Ingredients:
For the Chicken
- 40g dried apricots
- 1 large chicken
- 1 teaspoon za'atar
- Finely grated zest 1 lemon
- 300g couscous
- 50 g unsalted butter
- 1 teaspoon sumac
- 2 preserved lemons
- 25g flaked almonds
- Small handful mint
- 25g pomegranate seeds

For the Dressing
- 1 teaspoon tahini
- Juice ½ lemon
- 100g plain natural yogurt
- Small handful mint

- 1 medium cucumber

Method:
1. Preheat the oven to 190 degrees C.
2. Place the couscous in a small bowl and spill freshly filtered water over 450ml.
3. Then combine the preserved lemons, flaked almonds, fresh fruit, basil, and some spices with the fluff and a spoon.
4. In a shallow dish, combine the sugar, sumac, za'atar, lime zest, and some spice.
5. Fill the chicken cavity with the stored couscous thinly and place it, breast-side up, in the pan.
6. Fry till the meat is cooked through, and the flesh is crispy, for 1 hour 30 minutes to 1 hour 40 minutes.
7. Create the dressing, meantime. Mix the milk, cucumber, basil, tahini, lime juice, and spices in a shallow dish. Unless possible, cover and cool.
8. Strip the couscous filling from the cavity and platter until the poultry is fried and split between dishes.
9. Move the poultry and carve on a sheet. Split the chicken between the plates and rain the seasoning over it.

4.13 Lebanese Rice

Cooking Time: 15 minutes
Serving Size: 8
Ingredients:
- Dash cinnamon
- Parsley
- 2 cups long-grain white rice
- 2 tablespoons olive oil
- ½ teaspoon salt
- ½ cup vermicelli semolina

Method:

1. Till the water runs clean, wash the rice with ice water.
2. Well-drained and put aside.
3. Heat the oil in a large non-stick pot over medium heat.
4. Insert the spaghetti and steam the vermicelli, constantly stirring until all vermicelli is rich lightly browned.
5. Move the prepared vermicelli to the rice and mix to mix and cover the olive oil with the grain. If needed, sprinkle with salt and a splash of spices.
6. Transfer four cups of water to the combination and get it to a boil.
7. Lower the heat, cover the pan, and cook for fifteen minutes.
8. Turn off the heat when the rice is completely cooked and enable the rice to steam for five minutes.
9. Serve wet, if needed, with grated parmesan and toasted almonds.

4.14 Sumac Chicken Drumsticks with Tomato Spiced Salad

Cooking Time: 40 minutes
Serving Size: 4

Ingredients:

- 50-gram baby rocket leaves
- 2 tablespoon lemon juice
- ¾ cup fresh flat-leaf parsley
- ¼ cup fresh mint
- 20 chicken drumsticks
- 2 medium tomatoes
- 1 medium green capsicum
- ¼ cup sumac
- ½ Lebanese cucumber

- ¼ cup olive oil

Method:
1. Merge the sumac and poultry in a wide dish.
2. In a wide frying pan, cook poultry, warm two tablespoons of oil, seal, regularly rotating, until golden brown and cooked completely.
3. In the meantime, in a wide bowl with the cucumber, capsicum, herbs, tomato, rocket, and juices, put the remaining oils and toss completely.
4. Serve chicken and salads with it.

4.15 Lamb and Tabouli Open Wraps with Garlic Roasted Hummus

Cooking Time: 30 minutes
Serving Size: 4

Ingredients:
- 4 pieces Lebanese bread
- 200g roasted garlic hummus
- 1 teaspoon Moroccan seasoning
- 2 boneless lamb loin
- 90g cracked wheat
- ¼ cup spacious mint
- 1 tablespoon olive oil
- 1 tomato
- 2 spring onions
- 1 cup parsley
- 1 avocado
- 1 cucumber

Method:
1. Following the packet instructions, cook the crushed wheat.
2. Drain it and move it to a wide pan. Add peppers, cucumbers, avocado, green onions, kale, and parsley. Toss softly to mix and season.

3. In the meantime, preheat a nearly high barbecue.
4. Adjoin part of the oil and bowl of Moroccan spices. Arise to coat the sheep and insight.
5. Heat lower than moderate flame on top of a huge non-stick deep fryer.
6. Later on, coat the pan with oil.
7. Heat the lamb on either side for 2-3 minutes, moderate or until fried to your taste. Move to a dish.
8. Set it aside to rest for three minutes. Cut the lamb finely.
9. Brush a loaf of bread with one surface in the same method as a little steady oil.
10. Heat till the grill is sedated for two minutes or until softly toasted.
11. In style with one of the hummus, move back.
12. Continue in the same direction as the oil, hummus, bread, tabouli, and sheep that have remained.

Chapter 5: Lebanese Salad Recipes

5.1 Shangleesh Salad

Cooking Time: 10 minutes
Serving Size: 4
Ingredients:
- Freshly ground black pepper
- ½ lemon
- 500g Shangleesh Cheese
- ½ cup olive oil
- 1 tablespoon flat-leaf parsley
- 3 medium tomatoes
- ½ medium onion

Method:
1. Organize the tomatoes on a single sheet on a large pan.
2. Place a layer of crushed Shangleesh on top, followed by a sheet of onion, and finally parsley.
3. Sprinkle all the olive oil over it and press ½ of the lemon over it.
4. After this, give a small black pepper mixer.
5. You do not need any salt because the Shangleesh has all the salt that the dish requires.

5.2 Ham and Egg Salad

Cooking Time: 2 hours 20 minutes
Serving Size: 8
Ingredients:
- 2 tablespoons Dijon mustard
- Ground black pepper
- ½ cup dill pickle relish
- ¼ cup minced onion
- 4 slices ham

- 3 stalks celery
- 1 ½ cups light mayonnaise
- 4 hard-boiled eggs

Method:
1. Use the scraping blade of a mixing bowl to shred the ham.
2. In a big cup, stir together all the diced ham, sliced eggs, kale, mild mayo, and relish, ginger, Dijon mustard, and chili flakes.
3. Put it in the fridge for at least two hours before eating.

5.3 Chicken Shawarma Salad Bowls

Cooking Time: 1 hour 8 minutes
Serving Size: 4
Ingredients:
- 1 cup red onion
- 1 cup cucumber
- 2 pounds chicken breasts
- ½ cup lemon vinaigrette
- 1 cup cherry tomatoes
- ¼ cup olive oil
- 6 cups spring mix
- 2 tablespoons shawarma seasoning

Toppings
- Garlic tahini sauce
- Lemon tahini dressing
- Feta cheese crumbles
- Hummus
- Olives
- Pepperoncini's

Method:

1. Mix the chicken pieces with the vegetable oil and shawarma spices in a large mixing bowl until well covered in the coating.
2. Refrigerate the container for at least thirty minutes and up to four hours, wrapped with cling film.
3. Take the chicken from the marinade only after the chicken has braised and removed the braising liquid.
4. Use twelve skewers, slice 4-5 bits of chicken.
5. Heat the grill to a high temperature.
6. Roast the meat shawarma for four minutes on the one hand, then turn and cook for another four minutes.
7. Mix the tomatoes, spring onion, celery, and lime vinaigrette with the seasoning blend.
8. Separate the combination into four containers.
9. Cover it with Shawarma meat.

5.4 Fattoush Salad

Cooking Time: 15 minutes
Serving Size: 4

Ingredients:
Salad

- 2 green onions
- ¼ cup parsley
- ½ a large green pepper
- 5 radishes
- 1 large pita bread
- 1 large vine-ripe tomato
- 2-3 Persian cucumbers
- 3 tablespoon olive oil
- Freshly cracked pepper
- 1 large lettuce
- Kosher salt to taste

Dressing
- ½ teaspoon kosher salt
- Fresh cracked black pepper
- 1 teaspoon pomegranate molasses
- ½ teaspoon mint fresh
- 3 tablespoon olive oil
- 2 garlic cloves pressed
- 1 teaspoon grated lemon zest
- 2 tablespoon lemon juice

Method:
1. Warm three tablespoons of olive oil over medium-high heat in a pan.
2. Insert the flatbread and adjust coarse salt and freshly cracker peppers to the seasoning.
3. Cook the pita for five minutes until the bits are translucent in color and crispy.
4. Place back the flatbread.
5. In a big cup, combine olive oil, lime juice, ginger, cilantro, pomegranate molasses, basil, salt, and black pepper to the salad dressing supplies.
6. Mix when caramelized and well mixed with the coating.
7. The wide dressing pot introduces the cabbage, tomatoes, carrots, bell beans, radishes, fresh basil, and tarragon and tosses to blend.
8. Instantly before eating, add the crispy pita bread to the salads and mix it softly again.

5.5 Tabouli Salad Recipe

Cooking Time: 40 minutes
Serving Size: 6

Ingredients:
- ¼ cup mint leaves
- Salt and pepper to taste
- 2 vine-ripe firm tomatoes

- 2 green onions
- ⅓ cup extra-virgin olive oil
- ¼ cup extra-fine bulgur wheat
- 2 bunches parsley
- 3 tablespoons lemon juice

Method:
1. Mix all the vegetable oil and lime juice in a shallow saucepan until well mixed.
2. Then apply the bulgur to the coating and allow it to soak for about fifteen minutes, once soft and smooth.
3. In the meantime, wash and dry the veggies completely before finely slicing them.
4. In a wide jar, put the diced veggies in it. With salt and black pepper, spray.
5. Then spill over the combination of bulgur and dressing. Toss softly to mix.
6. If required, serve at ambient temperature or warm with lettuce.

5.6 Tangy Parsley and Lemon Beef Fattoush Salad

Cooking Time: 30 minutes
Serving Size: 4
Ingredients:
- Freshly ground black pepper
- 1-ounce feta cheese
- 1 clove garlic
- Kosher salt
- 1 tablespoon vegetable oil
- 1 tablespoon fresh lemon juice
- 1 teaspoon ground sumac
- ¾ cup fresh mint
- 2 tablespoons olive oil
- ½ red onion

- ¾ cup Italian parsley
- 2 small pita bread
- 3 cups halved grape tomatoes
- 1 large English cucumber

Method:
1. In a wide skillet, heat the cooking oil over moderate flame.
2. Fry once lightly browned in quantities and wipe dry with paper towels.
3. In a mixing dish, add cucumber, mint, red onion, tomatoes, parsley, olive oil, lime juice, cilantro, garlic, cinnamon, and black pepper.
4. Toss the salads with the crispy pita bits softly. Use the thin cheese grater to grind the grated feta cheese.

5.7 Fattoush Salad with Grilled Haloumi

Cooking Time: 30 minutes
Serving Size: 4

Ingredients:
- 7 oz. halloumi cheese
- 1 tablespoon za'atar
- Sea salt and
- Freshly cracked pepper
- 4 mini corn tortillas
- 3 tablespoon olive oil
- ½ bunch parsley
- 1 small lemon juiced
- 1 small garlic clove
- 2 tablespoon red onion
- ½ bunch fresh cilantro
- 1 large green bell pepper
- 1 Lebanese cucumber
- 2 large ripe tomatoes

Method:

1. Heat the pan on a barbecue over low heat.
2. Use a small volume of mist, deflate the tortilla chips.
3. Prepared pan on moderate flame and mist it with olive oil.
4. In the bowl, position one or two tortilla chips.
5. Heat for another 2-3 minutes before tossing.
6. Heat the tortilla for the next three minutes or until it is crispy.
7. The intention is for the tortilla to be toasted, so the bowl will not be too warm.
8. Repeat and switch off the fire with the leftover tortillas.
9. Once the tortillas are cool enough to manage, split them into bits and put them aside.
10. In a big cup, mix the bell pepper, peppers, cucumber, cabbage, coriander, tarragon, and garlic.
11. Sprinkle with lime juice and vegetable oil. To satisfy, sprinkle with salt.
12. On medium fire, preheat the same broiler pan.
13. When the pan is heated, add the halloumi strips and bake for two minutes on either hand before shifting them.
14. Organize the fried tortillas in small containers, then cover with lettuce and slices of halloumi. Spray and fill directly with za'atar.

5.8 Middle Eastern Style Fish with Chickpea Salad and Green Bean

Cooking Time: 10 minutes
Serving Size: 4

Ingredients:
Salad
- ¼ cup coriander leaves

- ¼ cup parsley
- 2 tomatoes
- 1 red onion
- 2 cucumbers

Dressing
- 1 garlic clove, smashed
- Salt and pepper
- ¼ cup extra virgin olive oil
- 1 teaspoon caster sugar
- 1½ tablespoon sherry vinegar
- 2 tablespoon lemon juice
- Zest of half a lemon

Chickpea spices
- 1 teaspoon ground cardamom
- ¼ teaspoon salt
- 1½ teaspoon All Spice
- 1 teaspoon ground cumin

Chickpeas
- 400g can chickpeas
- 2 tablespoon olive oil

Method:
1. Place the Coating components together in a pan.
2. To enable the flavors to grow, put them down for twenty minutes.
3. Chickpeas should be put in a large mixing bowl.
4. Disperse over the herbs, and then throw to cover.
5. In a wide skillet, steam 2 teaspoons olive oil over high temperature and fry the chickpeas for a few minutes.
6. Move the pot to roll up the chickpeas, or mix softly.
7. Place it in a cup and cool to room temperature.
8. In a mixing cup, mix the salad ingredients.
9. Toss with a little dressing drizzled on top. Put in a serving dish.

10.   Chickpeas should be sprinkled on top of the salad.
11.   Drizzle some more dressing on top.
12.   If needed, toss slightly. Serve right away.

Chapter 6: Lebanese Soup and Side Recipes

6.1 Meatball Fattoush

Cooking Time: 1 hour
Serving Size: 4

Ingredients:
- 1 small red onion, halved
- 1/3 cup parsley sprigs
- 200g cauliflower
- 1 tablespoon tahini
- 120g butter leaf blend
- 200g mixed medley tomatoes
- 1 tablespoon lemon juice
- 1 teaspoon finely grated lemon rind
- 2 pieces flatbread
- ½ cup Greek-style yogurt
- 560g packet beef and pork meatballs

Method:
1. Heat the oven to 200C.
2. In a large baking dish, put the cauliflower.
3. Squirt it with a spray of olive oil.
4. Preheat oven to 350°F and bake for 10 minutes.
5. In the oven, insert the tomatoes and bake for another ten minutes or until the tomato starts to collapse.
6. In the meantime, put the bread on a cookie sheet.
7. Squirt it with a spray of olive oil.
8. Preheat oven to 350°F and bake for five minutes, or until crispy.
9. Enable to cool before serving.
10. Put the meatballs on a tray and sprinkle with olive oil mist when the bread is frying.

11.   Over the moderate fire, heat a large deep fryer.
12.   Heat the meatballs, rotating, till the meatballs are heated through, or for eight minutes.
13.   In a shallow mixing cup, add the yogurt, lime juice, lime zest, tahini, and one tablespoon of sugar.
14.   Split the bread into tiny bits.
15.   Organize the lettuce leaves, onions, cabbage combination, and meatballs on a wide baking tray.
16.   Sprinkle the yogurt mixture on top. Serve with a tarragon garnish.

6.2 Broccolini Fattoush

Cooking Time: 25 minutes
Serving Size: 4

Ingredients:
- 1 garlic clove, crushed
- 1 teaspoon ground paprika
- 1 tablespoon olive oil
- 2 tablespoon lemon juice
- 1 large piece of Lebanese bread
- 350g mixed medley tomatoes
- ½ cup mint leaves
- Olive oil spray
- 175g packet minicabs
- 4 spring onions
- 1 bunch broccolini
- ½ bunch radishes
- 250g baby cucumbers

Method:
1. Preheat the boiler to 180C.
2. Put the bread on a cookie sheet and bake it.

3. Cook until crispy and dry, or for ten minutes.
4. Enable to cool before serving.
5. Cut into small bits. In the meantime, in a heatproof pan, put the broccolini.
6. Wrap and set it aside for two minutes with hot water. Drain the water.
7. In a cup, mix the broccolini, celery, parsnip, green onions, capsicum, tomato, spinach, and bread.
8. In a screw-top pot, combine the oil, lime juice, cloves, and paprika.
9. Shake once well mixed. Spoon the dressing over it.

6.3 Spiced Rosewater Apples

Cooking Time: 30 minutes
Serving Size: 4

Ingredients:
- 2 tablespoons lime juice
- Finely chopped pistachios
- 8 cardamom pods
- 2 tablespoons rosewater
- 900g white sugar
- 8 small apples
- 625ml water

Method:
1. In a medium bowl, concentrate the water and sugar.
2. Heat, mixing, till the sugar has melted over medium-high heat.
3. Add the apples and cardamom pods to the bowl. Just get it to a boil.
4. Reduce the heat to a low setting.
5. Boil for thirty minutes or until the apples are transparent. Set to chill.
6. Switch to a mixing platter or plate using a rubber spatula.

7. In the pot, boil the stored syrup for ten minutes over medium heat or thicker but not colored.
8. Sprinkle the warm syrup over the edge of the apples.

6.4 Za'atar Lamb Cutlet Platter with Dips

Cooking Time: 40 minutes
Serving Size: 6

Ingredients:
- 1 teaspoon dried oregano
- ½ teaspoon dried marjoram
- 1 teaspoon ground paprika
- 1 teaspoon dried thyme
- 18 lamb cutlets
- 1 tablespoon sesame seeds
- 2 teaspoons cumin seeds
- 200g hummus
- 200g eggplant dip
- 3 wholemeal pita bread
- Coriander leaves
- 200g beetroot dip
- 1 tablespoon olive oil

Method:
1. Heat the grill or barbecue to a moderate flame.
2. Merge the sesame oil, smoked paprika, parsley, dill, marjoram, and oregano in a large pan to make the za'atar.
3. In a large mixing bowl, position the lamb.
4. To mix, scatter over the za'atar and flip.
5. For moderate flame, grill on the barbecue for 2½ mins on either side.
6. Wrap in foil and move to a platter. Put aside to rest for five minutes.
7. In the meantime, spray the pita bread gently with grease.

8. Grill the pita bread for two minutes or until golden brown.
9. On a wide baking tray, place the lamb.
10. Garnish with cilantro. Offer with bread and sauces.

6.5 Beef, Fetta and Eggplant Parcels

Cooking Time: 40 minutes
Serving Size: 12

Ingredients:
- 1/3 cup Greek-style yogurt
- 1 tablespoon lemon juice
- 6 sheets frozen butter puff pastry
- 1 egg
- 1 ½ tablespoon olive oil
- 100g fetta
- 1/3 cup mint
- 1 brown onion
- ½ teaspoon chili flakes
- 500g beef mince
- 1 small eggplant
- 1 teaspoon ground coriander
- 2 garlic cloves

Method:
1. Preheat the boiler to 200C.
2. Heat the oil over moderate heat in a large deep fryer.
3. Cook, regularly mixing, for five minutes or until the onions and eggplant are tender.
4. Insert the flakes of garlic, cilantro, chili, fry, swirling, fand2 minutes.
5. Add the mince and simmer for five minutes or until golden brown, mixing with a spoon to break down any lumps.

6. Mix in the basil and fetta. Enable thirty minutes for cooling.
7. Use a thin paste to cover half the pastry balls, creating a 1cm border.
8. With half the shell, clean the surface.
9. Position the leftover pastry discs on top of the mince combination and lightly brush. Crimp the corners with a fork.
10.   Put the packets lined with baking parchment on two baking trays.
11.   Brush with the egg that remains.
12.   To add two small cuts on the top of each package, use a small, paring blade.
13.   Cook for 20 minutes, flipping trays midway through, until puffed and translucent.
14.   In the meantime, in a shallow pan, mix the yogurt and lime juice.
15.   Serve the parcels of salad leaves and citrus yogurt.

6.6 Lebanese Lentil Soup

Cooking Time: 50 minutes
Serving Size: 8

Ingredients:
- ½ cup chopped cilantro
- ¾ cup fresh lemon juice
- 1 tablespoon ground cumin
- ½ teaspoon cayenne pepper
- 1 tablespoon minced garlic
- 1 large onion, chopped
- 6 cups chicken stock
- 3 tablespoons olive oil
- 1 pound red lentils

Method:
1. In a medium skillet, take the chicken broth and lentils to a simmer at medium temperature.

2. Lower the temperature to moderate, cover, and cook for 20 minutes.
3. In the meantime, over moderate steam, heat the olive oil in a pan.
4. Add the garlic and onions and simmer for about three minutes till the onion has weakened and become transparent.
5. Mix the lentils with the vegetables and spice them with cumin and smoked paprika.
6. Cook for another ten minutes, or until the lentils are soft.
7. In a stand processor or with a food processor, gently puree the broth until creamy.
8. When eating, whisk in the cilantro and lime juice.

6.7 Lamb, Cinnamon and Pies Date Filo with Pistachio Honey Dressing

Cooking Time: 40 minutes
Serving Size: 4

Ingredients:
- 2 tablespoons pistachio kernels
- Salad leaves, to serve
- 2 tablespoons honey
- 1 tablespoon white balsamic vinegar
- 1½ tablespoons olive oil
- ½ teaspoon orange rind
- 12 sheets filo pastry
- 1 small red onion
- 60g dried dates, chopped
- 2 tablespoons orange juice
- 2 garlic cloves, crushed
- 1½ teaspoons ground cinnamon
- 500g lamb mince
- ½ teaspoon dried chili flakes
- 1 teaspoon ground cumin

Method:

1. In a deep fryer over moderate pressure, heat three tablespoons of the oil.
2. Heat the onion for three minutes, tossing, or until tender.
3. For two minutes, whisk in the ginger, cilantro, chili, and one teaspoon cinnamon.
4. Over moderate heat, heat the remaining liquid. Cook for four minutes until golden brown.
5. Combine the onion paste, dates, juices, and rind in a mixing bowl.
6. Sauté for 6 minutes, until the fluid has evaporated.
7. Put in a container and put aside for 10 minutes before serving.
8. Preheat oven to 350°F and bake for 20 minutes, or until golden brown.
9. In the meantime, over medium-high heat, mix the honey and mustard in a saucepan.
10. Stir till the honey melts for two minutes. Simmer for two minutes until the mixture thickens.
11. Stir the nuts in. Enable ten minutes for the sauce to thicken.

6.8 Lamb and Lemony Hummus Flatbreads

Cooking Time: 50 minutes
Serving Size: 4

Ingredients:

- Finely grated zest of ½ lemon
- Juice of ½ lemon
- ½ cup flat-leaf parsley
- ½ cup mint leaves
- 1 large flat focaccia
- 2 tablespoon red wine vinegar

- 2 green zucchini
- 1/3 cup extra virgin olive oil
- 1 small red onion
- 300g hummus
- 150g feta, crumbled
- 1 tablespoon za'atar
- 6 lamb sausages

Method:
1. Preheat the oven to 210 degrees Celsius.
2. Use baking parchment, cover a large sheet pan.
3. Put focaccia on a sheet cut-side up and place with hummus.
4. Spread crumbled sausage beef, feta, and za'atar on top.
5. Preheat the oven to 200°F and bake for twenty minutes.
6. Break the bits into four pieces.
7. In the meantime, in a shallow pan, mix the onion, vinegar, and a few salt flakes and put them aside for ten minutes.
8. Put zucchini, basil, lime juice, and zest, and the remaining two tablespoons of oil in a mixing bowl once ready to eat, season to taste, and mix to blend.
9. Serve pita bread topped with zucchini combination and soaked onion.

6.9 Caramel, Chocolate and Brownie Pie Almond Praline

Cooking Time: 1 hour 30 minutes
Serving Size: 12

Ingredients:
- ½ cup plain flour
- 1 tablespoon cocoa powder
- 1 egg, lightly beaten

- ½ cup caster sugar
- 75g butter
- 70g dark chocolate

Praline
- ¼ cup slivered almonds
- ¼ cup caster sugar

Pastry
- ½ cup slivered almonds
- 1 egg yolk
- 100g butter
- ¼ cup caster sugar
- 1 cup plain flour

Caramel
- 2 tablespoons golden syrup
- 2 tablespoons pure cream
- 395g can sweetened milk
- 50g butter

Method:
1. Preheat the boiler to 200C.
2. Combine the butter and starch.
3. Stir in the butter, egg white, and almonds. Softly knead until it's smooth.
4. In a shallow, deep fryer, heat the sugar for 5 minutes over medium-high heat or molten and softly translucent.
5. Toss in the almonds to cover. On a greased baking sheet, pour the mixture.
6. Cover with dry rice. For fifteen minutes, roast.
7. Drop the sheet and pie weights. Cook until translucent, or for ten minutes. Reduce the temperature of the oven to 180C.
8. Merge the butter, whipped cream, icing sugar, and cream over a moderate flame in a heavy-based frying pan.
9. Simmer for ten minutes or until the mixture turns translucent, stirring continuously.

10. Melt the butter over a moderate flame in a casserole bowl. Stir until sugar dissolves over high heat and add chocolate.
11. Withdraw from the heat. Stir in the milk, chocolate, and flour. Insert the almond praline and blend well.
12. Spread the combination of chocolate over a sheet of caramel.
13. Cook for approximately half an hour or until just strong. Serve after being refrigerated overnight.

6.10 Stuffed Zucchini

Cooking Time: 1 hour 10 minutes
Serving Size: 6

Ingredients:
For Stuffing
- Scant one teaspoon garlic powder
- Salt and pepper
- 2 tablespoon olive oil
- Scant one teaspoon allspice
- 1 can tomato with juice
- ½ cup water
- ½ cup long-grain rice
- ⅓ packed cup parsley
- ⅓ packed cup dill
- 1 small onion, shredded
- ½ lb. lean ground beef

For Zucchini
- 1 can tomato sauce
- ¾ cup water
- 1 small onion
- 2 ½ lb. zucchini
- 4 large tomatoes

Method:

1. Merge the components for the filling in a large dish.
2. Cut the vegetables.
3. The leftover tomato should be cut and scattered around the bottom of the plate.
4. Now insert the strips of the onions and the zucchini hearts. Season with a pinch of salt and pepper.
5. Then gently fill the flattened tomato with the rice filling, using your fingertips.
6. Insert the tomato sauces and water at this level. Season with a sprinkle of salt.
7. For half an hour, cover and boil until the zucchini is soft and the rice filling is thoroughly cooked.
8. Serve directly on a large plate.

6.11 Lamb with Hummus and Tabouli Platter

Cooking Time: 40 minutes
Serving Size: 4

Ingredients:
- Toasted pita bread and thick
- Greek-style yogurt, to serve
- Juice of ½ lemon
- 400g hummus
- 2 tablespoon olive oil
- 1 ½ cups beef stock
- Finely grated zest
- 1kg lamb leg steaks
- 1 onion
- 2 teaspoon ras el hanout
- 1 tbs tomato paste
- 2 garlic cloves

Tabbouleh
- Finely grated zest and
- Juice of ½ lemon
- 1 bunch coriander

- 1 bunch mint
- ½ cup burghul
- 1 Lebanese cucumber
- 2 tomatoes, seeds removed

Method:
1. Put burghul in a heat-proof cup for the tabbouleh and fill it with hot water.
2. Hold for twenty minutes.
3. In the meantime, warm oil in a deep frying pan on medium-high heat renders the flavored lamb.
4. Insert the meat, and bake until golden brown for 5-6 minutes. Add the onion and simmer for two minutes, swirling.
5. Add ras el hanout and cloves, then simmer for another two minutes until it's aromatic.
6. Add the tomato sauce and the reserved liquid.
7. Bring to a low boil, then decrease to medium heat and cook for ten minutes.
8. Stir in the lemon juice and zest, remove from the heat.
9. Wipe the burghul, then blend it with the remainder tabbouleh components in a mixing bowl, spice to taste, and stir to combine.
10. Create a well in the middle of a large dish with hummus, and whisk in the lamb.

6.12 Lebanese Vegetable Soup

Cooking Time: 35 minutes
Serving Size: 8

Ingredients:
- ¼ cup chopped fresh parsley
- 2 lemons, cut into wedges
- Ten artichoke hearts, cut into eighths
- ¾ cup canned chickpeas
- 1 large Spanish onion
- 4 -5 cups vegetable stock

- 2 large tomatoes, chopped
- 1½ cups chopped potatoes
- 1 teaspoon salt
- 2 tablespoons olive oil
- 2 ½ cups chopped carrots
- 1 teaspoon ground coriander
- 2 -4 garlic cloves, minced
- ¼ teaspoon ground red pepper

Method:

1. Five minutes in a big casserole dish, sauté the onions in the coconut oil.
2. Mix the carrot down. Cover with a sheet.
3. After three minutes, give it another swirl.
4. Add red peppers, cilantro, and garlic to the edge.
5. Heat for another few minutes wrapped.
6. Put the potatoes, salts, and half a cup of stock in the mixture.
7. Cover the pan and bring it to a boil with the broth.
8. Decrease the fire until the vegetables are almost soft and boil.
9. Make sure you don't overcook them.
10. Add the onions, artichoke cores, and chickpeas, stirring softly. Season with salt to compare.
11. Wrap and steam the vegetables for approximately 3 minutes, enough to steam them up.
12. Pour in the remainder 2-3 cups of stocks, or maybe more if you want a thicker soup. Warm on low heat.
13. Spray with grated parmesan on each plate and garnish with a piece of lemon.

6.13 Turkey Koftas with Couscous

Cooking Time: 10 minutes
Serving Size: 4

Ingredients:
- Olive oil spray
- 100g baby spinach leaves
- 1 teaspoon olive oil
- 330ml boiling water
- 500g Ingham turkey mince
- 2 teaspoons smoked paprika
- 240g couscous
- 50g garlic butter spread

Method:
1. Heat a moderate, flat barbecue pan.
2. In a mixing dish, mix the turkey, herbed butter, and red pepper.
3. Divide it into twelve sections. Form around the skewers.
4. In a heatproof dish, put the couscous. To mix, whisk in the water and oil.
5. Cover the bowl in cling film. Put aside for ten minutes. Split the grains with a fork.
6. Squirt oil on a flat pan.
7. Heat koftas for three minutes on either side or until heated through, rotating periodically.
8. Transfer the spinach and couscous leaf to the rocket. To mix, toss.

6.14 Shorbet Djaj - Chicken Soup

Cooking Time: 2 hours 15 minutes
Serving Size: 6

Ingredients:

- 3 tablespoons parsley
- Lemon juice
- 1 teaspoon salt
- ¼ teaspoon cinnamon
- 1400g chicken
- 250g rice
- 100g carrots
- 2 teaspoons salt
- 4 whole cardamom pods
- 2 bay leaves
- Half of a lemon
- 1 teaspoon salt
- 1 cinnamon stick
- 1 medium onion
- 2 liters cold water

Method:

1. Spray the poultry with two teaspoons salt and massage the half lime inside out.
2. Season the poultry with a teaspoon of salt.
3. In a big pot, add the meat and the broth, covers, and bring to the boil at high temperature.
4. Add the garlic, bay leaf, coriander seeds, and shallots to the pot.
5. Decrease the heat to medium-low and simmer for around 1 hour, sealed.
6. Throw out the carrot, bay leaf, pods of cardamom, and coriander seeds.
7. Place the chicken on a tray and set it aside.
8. Put the stock of chicken into a dry, large pot and keep it warm.

9. In a clean bowl, add chicken parts, along with the soaked rice and vegetables, sprinkle with salt and seasoning, and bring to a simmer.
10. Cover and cook for around fifteen minutes over medium-high heat. Serve instantly.

Conclusion

Almost anyone you know would have had a taste of Lebanese cuisine. From the Mid-East to New Zealand, through Asia and Europe, eventually landing in the Americas. This cuisine has acquired a special location on all continents. The recipe has a long tradition that goes back to ancient times. It is also colored by the various hues of cultures that have inhabited its lovely property. Good eating is the rule, and not just in the country's capital of Beirut, but in all countries, many restaurants offer delicious dishes. As the baked goods are often filled with veggies or the veggies are stuffed with beef, Lebanese food has distinctive ways of preparing.

The traditional Lebanese meal begins with "mezze," which is a salad and nut mixture. The food is cooked with great care, and the Lebanese dishes are displayed in a very clean and artistic way. Lebanese cuisine is a gastronomic meal due to its careful cooking and clean appearance. Any place's food signifies a lot about the people's culture and lifestyle, and the Lebanese food is very controlled. They invoke a lot about Lebanon-Culture and Society. Even though Lebanese cuisine has developed over time, it has still closely related to its origins and historical influences. You have arrived at the right spot if you are trying to experience one of the tastiest and most enjoyable cuisines in the world. Try these recipes and garnish your meals with the healthiest ingredients.

The Pescatarian Cookbook

Follow a healthier lifestyle, lose weight and plan your meals and diet with over 100 recipes to learn how to cook seafood and fish.

By

Adele Tyler

The trademarks that are used are without any consent, and the publication of the trademark is without permission or backing by the trademark owner. All trademarks and brands within this book are for clarifying purposes only and are the owned by the owners themselves, not affiliated with this document.

Table of contents

Introduction

In the current world, we as humans have become very conscious of our health. We mostly prefer organic diet over other artificially grown foods. Being on a diet has been the most popular answer we get whenever we ask someone about their health. It is a very famous saying that, "your health is directly proportional to your mood swings," if you eat healthy and eat right, you are always going to have a splendid and wonderful mood.

This book is a road map towards eating different and eating healthy. While, losing weight vegetarians feel the most difficulty as they lack the essential amino acid source in their diet. Pescatarians on the other hand are vegetarians but those who fill their essential protein source with the help of seafood in their diet.

In this book, you will learn everything about the Pescatarian diet, the history, and the origin of this diet. You will come across various benefits of adopting this dieting regime, and the overall effect of seafood on your health in the chapters of this book. There are also other dietetic plans that people adopt very often such as the Carnivore diet and the Vegetarian diet. You will learn the difference between all the three diets, and acquire the knowledge of the advantages, and disadvantages of all these diet plans.

Moving towards the main part of the book, the shopping list that you need to start your diet plan is also provided along with a sample meal plan that will assist you in making your own diet routine. Hundred recipes including breakfast, lunch, dinner, snacks, sweet dishes, and juices are mentioned in this cookbook that are very easy to make on your own in your kitchen. So, why wait further when you can get healthy starting from today, let us dive into the pool of health together.

Chapter 1: Introduction to Pescatarian Diet

A Pescatarian is somebody who decides to eat a veggie diet; however who likewise eats fish, and other seafood products. It is a generally plant based eating regimen of whole grains, nuts, vegetables, whole produce, and solid fats, with fish assuming a key function as a principle protein source. Numerous Pescatarians likewise eat dairy and eggs.

Obviously, similarly as vegan diets can vary broadly, so can Pescatarian ones. It is conceivable to eat a meat free diet that is brimming with processed starches, junk food items and fish sticks, as opposed to a more advantageous one dependent on whole food sources.

1.1 History and Origins of Pescatarian Diet

The word vegetarian is defined by the Oxford Dictionary as 'a person who does not eat meat or fish, and sometimes other animal products, especially for moral, religious, or health reasons.' While this is a good broad definition of the vegetarian diet, the actual practice of vegetarianism is somewhat less clear cut.

There are several subcategories of vegetarianism including Ovolactarians, who eat dairy products, and eggs but abstain from meat, and Lactarians, who eat dairy products but abstain from meat and eggs. Some people include fish in their diet but still consider themselves vegetarians; a new name for this lifestyle, Pescatarian, has recently emerged. Vegans are the strictest subcategory of the vegetarian movement, abstaining from all animal-based products. Strict followers of veganism do not eat honey, or wear leather, or wool. While religion sometimes calls for a vegetarian or vegan diet, over the years we have seen an increasing number of individuals choosing not to consume animal products based on their personal beliefs.

A portion of the principal self-announced Vegetarians were the Pythagoreans, a title got from the Greek logician Pythagoras, a founder of the mathematical Pythagorean hypothesis. In spite of the fact that Pythagoras lent his name to the meatless eating routine, it is muddled whether he followed a severe vegan routine or not. Some people speculate that along with a typical breakfast of nectar, and supper of grain bread with vegetables, he may have eaten fish also, which would have made him Pescatarian by the present principles.

Supporters of Pythagoras received his dietary limitations, accepting that they were useful in helping life span. The lessons of Pythagorus were first distributed in quite a while by Italian essayist, and Doctor Antonio Cocchi; in 1745 they were converted into English by Robert Dodsley. A record of his eating regimen additionally showed up in the Greek thinker Porphyry's book *On Abstinence from Animal Food* (third century). The compelling chronicled archive incorporates a portion of exactly the same contentions that cutting edge vegans use while lauding the benefits of a meatless eating regime. With vegetarianism on the rise, it is now common for restaurants to feature vegetarian menus, or meatless entrée alternatives. Grocery stores carry a large variety of vegetarian options, proving a strong market for meatless products. With proper attention to nutritional intake, it is entirely possible for vegetarians, and vegans to live a long and healthy life.

1.2 Benefits of Pescatarian Diet in terms of Nutrition

In the Pescatarian diet, a person's main source of animal protein comes from fish, and other seafood, such as shrimp etc. Eating a diet consisting mainly of plant-based foods has a variety of health benefits, which the addition of fish and fish products may enhance. However, some types of fish may absorb mercury from their environment, so certain people may need to limit their intake. Following are some benefits of the Pescatarian diet in terms of Nutrition:

1. A Pescatarian diet may ensure individual's safety against colorectal diseases, or malignancies that influence the colon, and rectum. As indicated by a recent report, colorectal malignant growths are the subsequent driving reason for disease passing in the United States. The examination utilized information

from a companion of more than 77,650 individuals, and found that the Pescatarian diet had a solid defensive impact against colorectal malignant growths.

2. Following a plant-based eating routine can diminish the danger of type-2 diabetes, and metabolic disorder. Metabolic disorder incorporates conditions, for example, insulin opposition, hypertension, and heftiness. There is likewise proof that omega-3s present in greasy fish may diminish aggravation, however this proof originates from preliminaries of enhancements. Plant-based eating regimens are high in calming, and cell reinforcement operators, for example, flavonoids. Flavonoids have a scope of calming, and antidiabetic properties.

3. Some people choose vegetarian diets because they disagree with factory farming practices, or killing animals for food. For people concerned about animal welfare, the Pescatarian diet may be a little more suitable. This is because some scientists argue that fish cannot feel pain.

4. Eating fish, especially fatty fish, provides increased long-chain omega-3 fatty acid intake. An omega-3 fatty acid is an unsaturated fat that can be beneficial to people, and some omega-3s are integral for healthy living. People who eat fish have lower blood pressure, a lower risk of abnormal heart rhythms, and fewer fatal heart attacks than those who do not include fish in their diet.

5. Plant-based diets can help a person maintain a healthy weight, and they also may help with weight loss when necessary. A Pescatarian diet may also be more healthful than some diets that rely on calorie deficits to reduce weight.

1.3 Effects of Seafood on Overall Health of an Individual

The foods we eat influence our health. Besides containing protein, and other nutrients such as vitamin D and selenium, fish (either finfish or shellfish) contain a specific type of fat, omega-3 fatty acids, that may reduce the risk of developing heart disease, and other medical problems.

Omega-3 fatty acids are found in fish especially oily fish such as salmon, sardines, and herring. These omega-3 fatty acids can help lower your blood pressure, lower your heart rate, and improve other cardiovascular risk factors. Eating fish reduces the risk of death from heart disease, the leading cause of death in both men, and women. Fish intake has also been linked to a lower risk of stroke, depression, and mental decline with age. For pregnant women, mothers who are breastfeeding, and women of childbearing age, fish intake is important because it supplies DHA, a specific omega-3 fatty acid that is beneficial for the brain development of infants.

Fishes help keep up cardiovascular wellbeing by assuming a function in the guideline of blood thickening, and vessel choking, and are significant for pre-birth and postnatal neurological turn of event. Fish may lessen tissue irritation, and ease the manifestations of rheumatoid joint pain, and may assume a valuable part in cardiovascular arrhythmia (unpredictable heartbeat), lessening sadness, and ending mental decrease in more established individuals.

Chapter 2: Comparison of Pescatarian Diet with Other Diets

Many healthy eaters are reducing their intake of meat, and other animal products to boost wellness. If you are considering different options, there are many different plant based eating plans to choose from. The Pescatarian diet is just one of them.

In this chapter you will see how the Pescatarian diet is different from the Vegetarian, and Carnivore diet.

2.1 Pescatarian Diet vs. Carnivore Diet

Being a Pescatarian is where you eat meat, but only meat that comes from the sea. Fish has a lot of iron in it, and that can benefit your health greatly. Plus, it is easier to be cruelty free when it comes to. A great way to become a Pescatarian is by finding a great local fish market near you.

The biggest benefit includes the iron that fish have, the more fish you eat, the greater amount of iron you will have. Just as well, you will not be consuming land animals, so you will be more conscious when it comes to those types of meat. The downside is the price. Fish is more expensive, so you will have to work around that. Also, fish has a ton of mercury in it, so you will have to make sure to maintain that.

If you want to become more animal product conscious, but do not want to give up meat entirely, the carnivore diet is probably the way to go for you. You can do this by being aware of where your animal products are coming from. Happy farms are the best way to think about doing this. An animal without a bunch of hormones injected in is going to be great for you. Furthermore, cage-free animals are happier. Animal cruelty free meat is a major thing. Knowing where my meat is coming from makes you feel really good. Some farm animals do not ever see sunlight, let alone get to roam around.

Weight Loss

The Pescatarian diet may cause weight loss when portions are controlled while the Carnivore diet also cause the same effect of weight loss but unfortunately there is a drawback of not getting the proper nutrients the body needs that comes from plant based diets.

Health Risks

Carnivore diets come with nutritional deficiencies that can be a cause of big health risks for any individuals in the future. On the other hand one specific risk associated with a Pescatarian diet is the presence of mercury or heavy metals, a registered dietician. Fish, shellfish, and other seafood accumulate mercury in their bodies. As bigger fish eat smaller fish, this can drive up the concentration of these potentially dangerous toxins in the flesh of the larger fish.

Health Benefits

Carnivore, and Pescatarian both diets are very healthy for individuals, and they provide us a variety of nutrients that are unlikely to occur in the case of carnivore diets that lack plants on the whole and so lack all the nutrients that occur in plant based diets.

2.2 Pescatarian Diet vs. Vegetarian Diet

There are no exact rules that figure out what is a Pescatarian, and what is a Vegetarian. Furthermore, there are no guidelines that characterize how frequently you have to eat fish so as to be a Pescatarian. For instance, you might be a vegan who once in a while eats fish or you may remember it for each dinner. Nutritionists state that Pescatarians will in general be individuals who are wellbeing cognizant, and settle on careful decisions when arranging dinners. They might be people who are thinking about a vegan diet, and are utilizing a fish-based way to deal with plant-based eating. Or on the other hand they might be individuals who intend to follow a Pescatarian diet as long as possible, to dodge red meat.

Health Risks

One specific risk associated with a Pescatarian diet is the presence of mercury or heavy metals. Fish, shellfish, and other seafood accumulate mercury in their bodies. As bigger fish eat smaller fish, this can drive up the concentration of these potentially dangerous toxins in the flesh of the larger fish.

Overall Cost

Both Vegetarian and Pescatarian diets can be budget-friendly, especially if you are including conventionally grown products instead of seeking out only organic items.

The addition of seafood in a Pescatarian diet could increase the cost, but choosing canned and frozen options, especially when they are on sale, can help reduce the cost. Red meat, and poultry can be expensive, so forgoing these purchases in favor of more fresh fruits and vegetables, whole grains, legumes and fish could reduce your overall shopping bill. As with any diet, the quality of the food is also important. Look for whole, unprocessed options rather than prepackaged or prepared foods. These whole foods that you cook yourself are usually less expensive than prepared foods.

Health Benefits

Both diets are considered majorly plant based. The people who are following these diets will achieve many of the benefits associated with plant based diets. This approach to eating when done right has been associated with plenty of health benefits including better control of blood pressure, better control of blood glucose, less inflammation, reduced cholesterol levels. These factors translate into improved heart health, a reduced risk of developing diabetes and a reduced risk of certain types of cancer.

Additionally Pescatarians have the added benefit of getting plenty of omega-3 fatty acids, which are known for their heart-protective and anti-inflammatory properties. Omega-3s are essential compounds that the body cannot make on its own. You have to ingest them as part of your diet or in supplement form. They are critical to maintaining cardiovascular health. Fatty fish, such as sardines, mackerel and salmon are rich sources of omega-3s.

Weight Loss

The Pescatarian diet may cause weight loss when portions are controlled while the Vegetarian diet also cause the same effect of weight loss if the portion size of the meals are quantified properly.

Conclusion

Both the Pescatarian and Vegetarian diets can be perfectly healthy diets. These diets focus on eating whole, unprocessed foods rather than packaged junk foods. It all comes down to which foods you are choosing and whether you are covering all your needs. You need a variety of vitamins and minerals to fulfil your daily requirement. One area where Pescatarian diets might have a leg up over strictly Vegetarian diets is in providing more omega-3 fatty acids.

Chapter 3: Pescatarian Diet- Shopping List and Meal Plan

The Pescatarian diet originates from a Vegetarian diet, zeroing in on plant-based nourishments and fish, however dispensing with meat and poultry. Numerous individuals decided to turn into a Pescatarian on the grounds that it considers a smoother change to a plant-based eating routine and can be simpler to support in the drawn out when contrasted with a Vegetarian diet. In addition, fish is a finished wellspring of protein and has a large number of dietary advantages. Most Pescatarians like eggs and dairy for their eating routine, however some do not as this is an individual decision.

3.1 Grocery List- Foods You Need To Follow the Diet

Following is the grocery list that you need to follow before starting your Pescatarian diet:

- Beans and legumes
- All kinds of fish
- Tofu and tempeh
- Chia seeds
- All kinds of nuts
- Flax seeds
- Shellfish
- All kinds of fruits
- All kinds of vegetables
- Dairy products
- Eggs
- Brown rice
- Oatmeal
- Quinoa
- Different sauces: oyster sauce, chili sauce, soy sauce, Worcestershire sauce
- Whole wheat flour or bread
- Dried spices and mix herbs
- Different oils: canola oils, olive oil, sunflower oil

3.2 7 Day Sample Meal Plan of Pescatarian Diet

Day 1:

Breakfast: Scrambled eggs with cheese
125 kcalories

Lunch: Lemon kale and salmon pasta
186 kcalories

Snack: Green tea smoothie
183 kcalories

Dinner: Buckwheat pasta salad
402 kcalories

Total Calories
896 kcalories

Day 2:

Breakfast: Egg muffin
105 kcalories

Lunch: Caesar salad
186 kcalories

Snack: Black current and kale smoothie
183 kcalories

Dinner: Prawn Arabiata
434 kcalories

Total Calories
908 kcalories

Day 3:

Breakfast: Tomato Omlette
125 kcalories

Lunch: Caribbean Salad with shrimp
192 kcalories

Snack: Strawberry and cucumber juice
183 kcalories

Dinner: Miso marinated cod with stir-fried greens
450 kcalories

Total Calories
950 kcalories

Day 4:

Breakfast: Date and Walnut Oatmeal
350 kcalories

Lunch: Tofu and kale pesto sandwich
186 kcalories

Snack: Green tea smoothie
183 kcalories

Dinner: Prawn Arabiata
420 kcalories

Total Calories
1139 kcalories

Day 5:

Breakfast: Banana Egg pancakes
125 kcalories

Lunch: Caesar salad
186 kcalories

Snack: Mango and Pineapple smoothie
183 kcalories

Dinner: Lemon kale salmon pasta
620 kcalories

Total Calories
1122 kcalories

Day 6:

Breakfast: Blueberry pancakes
509 kcalories

Lunch: Potato soup
186 kcalories

Snack: Green Juice
143 kcalories

Dinner: New Orleans
416 kcalories

Total Calories
1251 kcalories

Day 7:

Breakfast: Oat and berry Acai bowl
501 kcalories

Lunch: Shrimp Coronation salad
186 kcalories

Snack: Melon and Grape Juice
125 kcalories

Dinner: Baked salmon with mint dressing
350 kcalories

Total Calories
1162 kcalories

The above designed diet plans are made from the same recipes which are listed in the chapters below, and you can indulge variations into your meal plans according to your choices.

Chapter 4: Pescatarian Diet Recipes

The only thing worse than a bad meal is no meal at all. Luckily, that is not going to be an issue for you. Following are a lineup of some of the best Pescatarian meal ideas in this chapter. Each recipe is genuinely tasty, easy to make and nutritious.

4.1 Breakfast Recipes

1) Caramelized Banana Dark Chocolate Oatmeal

Preparation time: 10 minutes

Cooking Time: 10 minutes

Serving: 1

Ingredients:

- Olive oil spray
- Water, one cup
- Sliced medium banana, half
- Dark chocolate chips, two tbsp.
- Rolled oats, one cup

Instructions:

1. In a small saucepan, bring water to a boil.
2. Stir in oats and reduce heat to low.
3. Simmer until oats have absorbed all of the liquid, three to five minutes.
4. While oats are cooking, spray a small non-stick skillet with olive oil.
5. Add sliced bananas in a single layer and cook over medium heat until caramelized, about three minutes per side.
6. Spoon oatmeal into a bowl and top with caramelized bananas, and chocolate chips.

2) Scrambled Eggs with Cheese

Preparation time: 5 minutes

Cooking Time: 12 minutes

Serving: 4-6

Ingredients:

- Mozzarella cheese, one cup
- Butter, three tbsp.
- Salt and Pepper, to taste
- Eggs, twelve

Instructions:

1. In a large nonstick pan with sloped sides, melt the butter over medium-low heat, being careful to not brown the butter.
2. If it begins to bubble, the heat is too high, so lower the heat to cook the eggs properly.
3. Meanwhile, in a large bowl, add the eggs and one teaspoon cold water.
4. Vigorously whisk until frothy and smooth.
5. Swirl the pan around to coat the butter on the bottom and up the sides.
6. Pour the eggs into the pan and let sit for a few seconds.
7. When the eggs begin to lightly set on the bottom, use the whisk to gently beat the eggs, and then allow them to sit for just a few seconds between beating them again.
8. Curds will begin to form and increase throughout the cooking time. Repeat this process of whisking then resting the eggs for a few seconds until about 50 percent of the eggs are set and the rest are still wet.
9. At this point, sprinkle the eggs with a pinch of salt and pepper and continue to whisk and rest alternately.
10. Once the eggs are 75 percent done add the cheese and from this moment, continue to whisk the eggs until done. This entire process from pouring in the eggs to them being finished should take eight minutes.
11. Remove from the heat and continue to scramble in the last seconds.
12. Your dish is ready to be served.

3) Breakfast Egg Muffins

Preparation time: 10 minutes

Cooking Time: 40 minutes

Serving: 12

Ingredients:

- Yellow onion chopped, one
- Turkey bacon, three slices
- Cooking spray
- Salt and Pepper, to taste
- Eggs, six
- Chopped red bell pepper, one
- Shredded mozzarella cheese, half cup
- Chopped baby spinach, one cup
- Garlic powder, half tsp.
- Paprika, half tsp.
- Milk, three tbsp.

Instructions:

1. Preheat oven to 350° and grease a 12-cup muffin tin with avocado or coconut oil cooking spray or coconut oil.
2. In a large nonstick skillet over medium heat, cook turkey bacon until crispy, six and eight minutes.
3. Drain on a paper towel-lined plate, then crumble.
4. Add onion and bell pepper to skillet and cook until soft. Cook for approximately five minutes.
5. Add spinach and cook until wilted, two minutes more.
6. In a small bowl, whisk eggs, milk, paprika, and garlic powder and season with salt and pepper.

7. Fold in cooked vegetable mixture, turkey bacon, and mozzarella. Pour mixture into prepared muffin tin.
8. Bake until cooked through and golden for thirty minutes.
9. Your dish is ready to be served.

4) Chickpea Flour Pancakes

Preparation time: 5 minutes

Cooking Time: 5 minutes

Serving: 2

Ingredients:
- Water, one cup
- Olive oil, one tbsp.
- Cooking spray
- Salt and Pepper, to taste
- Chickpea flour, one cup
- Spring onions, one cup
- Chili flakes, half tsp.
- Turmeric, half tsp.
- Peas, half cup
- Chopped red bell peppers, half cup

Instructions:
1. Add the flour, water, turmeric, salt, pepper and chili flakes to a mixing bowl and give it a quick blend using a food processor or blender.
2. Leave it to settle for a few minutes while you heat up the oil or ghee in a non-stick pan.
3. The batter needs to look very runny.

4. Dice the veggies finely and add them to the mixture.
5. Use a tissue or similar to ensure the bottom of the pan is coated well in oil.
6. Add about a ladle of the mixture and veggies when the pan is hot a medium heat should be just right.
7. Cook for about three minutes the mixture will quickly start to firm.
8. If you are using two pans, you can make two pancakes at the same time.
9. Make sure you use a large pan here, you are aiming for thin pancakes.
10.   Use a large spatula to help you flip the pancakes, adding more oil underneath if necessary.
11.   Your pancakes are ready to serve.

5) Dutch Banana Pancakes

Preparation time: 5 minutes

Cooking Time: 5 minutes

Serving: 2

Ingredients:

- Milk, half cup
- Flour, half cup
- Cooking spray
- Eggs, three
- Sugar, one tbsp.
- Nutmeg, half tsp.
- Butter, two tbsp.
- Sliced banana, one

Instructions:

1. Mix all the ingredients together and make a smooth batter.
2. Make sure you use a large pan here; you are aiming for perfect pancakes.
3. Use a large spatula to help you flip the pancakes, adding more butter underneath if necessary.
4. Your pancakes are ready to serve.

6) Rubab Mango Oatmeal

Preparation time: 5 minutes

Cooking Time: 5 minutes

Serving: 1

Ingredients:

- Orange juice, half cup
- Oats, one cup
- Fresh rhubarb, one cup
- Milk, one and a half cup
- Salt, a pinch
- Brown sugar, three tbsp.
- Cinnamon, half tsp.
- Chopped pecans or any nuts, two tbsp.
- Chopped mango slices, one

Instructions:

1. Combine milk, juice, oats, rhubarb, cinnamon and salt in a medium saucepan. Bring to a boil over medium-high heat.

2. Reduce heat, cover and cook at a very gentle bubble, stirring frequently, until the oats and rhubarb are tender, about five minutes.
3. Remove from the heat and let stand, covered, for five minutes.
4. Stir in sweetener to taste.
5. Garnish with nuts and mango slices.

7) Easy Tomato Omelet

Preparation time: 5 minutes

Cooking Time: 5 minutes

Serving: 1

Ingredients:
- Fresh basil, half cup
- Spring onions, half cup
- Cherry tomatoes, half cup
- Eggs, two
- Salt, a pinch
- Red chili
- Pepper, half tsp.

Instructions:
1. Wash the tomatoes, chilies, and spring onion and chop into small pieces.
2. Heat half the oil in a pan and fry the tomatoes for about two minutes.
3. Set aside.
4. Clean the pan with a tissue.
5. Crack the eggs into a bowl and beat well with a fork, adding the salt and pepper

6. Heat the rest of the oil in a pan on low to medium heat.
7. Pour the egg mix into the pan.
8. Using a spatula, ruffle the omelet so it does not stick.
9. As you create gaps tilt the pan so the liquid fills the spaces.
10. Let it cook for about two minutes and when the egg mixture looks nearly cooked drop on the tomatoes and basil.
11. Fold the empty half of the omelet on top of the other.
12. Slide it onto a plate the heat from closing the omelet will finish cooking the inside.
13. Your dish is ready to be served.

8) Breakfast Burrito

Preparation time: 15 minutes

Cooking Time: 15 minutes

Serving: 4

Ingredients:

- Wheat tortillas, four
- Chopped red onions, half cup
- Red bell pepper, half cup
- Black beans, one cup
- Eggs, four
- Hot sauce
- Salt, a pinch
- Canola oil, one tbsp.
- Red chili, one tbsp.
- Pepper, half tsp.
- Sour cream, half cup

- Shredded mozzarella cheese, one cup
- Chopped tomato, half cup
- Chopped avocado, half cup

Instructions:

1. Heat the canola oil in a large nonstick skillet over a medium-high heat.
2. Cook the onions and peppers until onions are softened and peppers are slightly charred, about eight minutes.
3. Add black beans and red pepper flakes and cook until warmed through, another three minutes.
4. Season with salt and pepper and transfer to a dish.
5. Whisk together the eggs and egg whites then stir in the cheese.
6. Spray the skillet with cooking spray, and reheat the skillet over a medium heat. Reduce heat to low and add eggs, scrambling until cooked through, about three minutes.
7. Spread each tortilla with one tablespoon each sour cream and salsa, then layer with some of the black bean mixture, some of the scrambled eggs, some diced tomato and some of the avocado.
8. Season, to taste, with hot sauce.
9. Roll up burrito-style and serve hot.

9) The Runner's Sandwich

Preparation time: 5 minutes

Cooking Time: 5 minutes

Serving: 1

Ingredients:

- Bread, four slices
- Olives, half cup
- Sun dried tomatoes, half cup
- Capers, two tbsp.
- Fresh basil, half cup
- Salt, a pinch
- Canola oil, one tbsp.
- Red chili, one tbsp.
- Pepper, half tsp.
- Oregano, half tsp.
- Shredded mozzarella cheese, one cup

Instructions:

1. Roughly chop the cheese, tomatoes, olives and capers and throw into a mixing bowl.
2. Add the herbs, salt and pepper.
3. Use a fork to mix up and mash the ingredients a little not too much.
4. If you are using very soft bread then pop it in the toaster or pan without oil for a minute or so not to toast it, just to harden the outside.
5. If the bread is already a hard type.
6. Spread the mix on the bottom slices; add the other slices on top.
7. Squish down.
8. Heat the pan and put the sandwich in.
9. Put a lid on the pan.
10. Cook for three to four minutes, squishing down with a spatula occasionally, then flip and cook the other side the same way.
11. Both outsides should be nice and crispy, the insides melting together.
12. Your sandwich is ready to be served.

10)   Banana Egg Pancakes

Preparation time: 5 minutes

Cooking Time: 10 minutes

Serving: 6

Ingredients:

- Baking powder, two tsp.
- Coconut flour powder six tbsp.
- Ripe banana, two
- Vanilla extracts, one tsp.
- Eggs, two
- Oil
- Maple syrup
- Fresh berries
- Coconut yogurt
- Seeds
- Nut butter

Instructions:

1. To a large mixing bowl, add bananas and mash until only small bits remain.
2. Then add baking powder and vanilla extract and use a fork or whisk to mash until thoroughly combined.
3. Next add eggs, break yolks with a fork or whisk, and whisk thoroughly until well combined.
4. Lastly, add coconut flour one tbsp. at a time until a thick but scoopable batter is achieved.
5. If you add too much coconut flour, add a little dairy free milk to thin.
6. Heat a large skillet over medium heat.
7. Once hot, add a little cooking oil to coat the pan.
8. Then spoon in roughly three tbsp. amounts of batter and reduce heat to low. These benefit from

cooking slower and lower than your average pancakes. Cover with a lid to help the center cook through.

9. Cook for three to four minutes, then remove lid and flip carefully.
10. Transfer cooked pancakes to the preheated oven on the prepared baking sheet.
11. To serve, top with desired toppings, such as nut butter, sliced bananas or fresh fruit, dairy-free yogurt, or maple syrup.

11) Coffee Chia Pudding

Preparation time: 5 minutes

Cooking Time: 10 minutes

Serving: 2

Ingredients:

- Almond milk, one cup
- Vanilla extract, one tsp.
- Maple syrup, one tbsp.
- Whipped cream
- Coffee, powder, one tbsp.
- Chia seeds, half cup

Instructions:

1. Combine all the things together except the whipped cream.
2. Serve them in a bowl and top with whipped cream.
3. Your dish is ready to be served.

12) Eggs in a Cloud

Preparation time: 10 minutes

Cooking Time: 10 minutes

Serving: 2

Ingredients:

- Salt, one pinch
- Mixed cheese, half cup
- Eggs, two

Instructions:

1. Preheat the oven to 450 degrees with a rack in the middle.
2. Line a roasting pan, or baking sheet that can take high temperatures without warping, with parchment paper.
3. Separate the egg yolks from the whites.
4. Make sure there are no little pieces of egg yolk in the whites or you will have difficulty getting the whites to beat properly.
5. It helps if you are making more than one egg nest to keep each egg yolk in a separate prep bowl.
6. Place the egg whites in a very clean mixer bowl.
7. Add a small pinch of salt to the egg whites.

8. Beat the egg whites with a whisk attachment in a mixer, starting on low speed and then slowly increasing to high speed, until stiff peaks form.
9. Your dish is ready to be served.

13) Buttermilk Pancakes

Preparation time: 10 minutes

Cooking Time: 10 minutes

Serving: 4

Ingredients:

- Salt, one pinch
- All-purpose flour, two cup
- Eggs, two
- Unsalted butter, three tbsp.
- Sugar three tbsp.
- Baking powder, one tsp.
- Baking soda, one tsp.
- Buttermilk, two cups
- Canola oil, for cooking

Instructions:

1. Heat the oven to 325 degrees.
2. Whisk flour, sugar, baking powder, baking soda and kosher salt together in a bowl.
3. Using the whisk, make a well in the center.
4. Pour the buttermilk into the well and crack eggs into buttermilk.
5. Pour the melted butter into the mixture.
6. Starting in the center, whisk everything together, moving towards the outside of the bowl, until all ingredients are incorporated.

7. Heat a large nonstick griddle or skillet, preferably cast-iron, over low heat for about five minutes.
8. Add one tablespoon oil to the skillet.
9. Turn heat up to medium low and using a measuring cup, ladle the batter into the skillet.
10. Flip pancakes after bubbles rise to surface and bottoms brown, about two minutes. Cook until the other sides are lightly browned.
11. Remove pancakes to a wire rack set inside a rimmed baking sheet, and keep in heated oven until all the batter is cooked and you are ready to serve.

14)   Baked Eggs with Spinach and Tomatoes

Preparation time: 10 minutes

Cooking Time: 10 minutes

Serving: 4

Ingredients:

- Salt, one pinch
- Eggs, four
- Chili flakes, three tbsp.
- Butter, one tsp.
- Chopped tomatoes, two cups
- Spinach, one cup

Instructions:

1. Heat oven to 200 degrees.
2. Put the spinach into a colander, and then pour over a kettle of boiling water to wilt the leaves.
3. Squeeze out excess water and divide between four small ovenproof dishes.
4. Mix the tomatoes with the chili flakes and some seasoning, then add spinach while shifting the material in dishes.
5. Make a small well in the center of each and crack in an egg.
6. Bake for ten mins or more depending on how you like your eggs.
7. Serve with crusty bread.

15)   Almond and Cherry Oatmeal

Preparation time: 5 minutes

Cooking Time: 5 minutes

Serving: 4

Ingredients:

- Dried oats, half cup
- Vanilla almond milk, three cups
- Salt, a pinch
- Cherries, one cup

Instructions:

1. Stir together oats, almond milk, and salt in a large microwave safe bowl.
2. Microwave on high for five minutes, stirring every two minutes, until oats are soft and most of the liquid has been absorbed.

3. Stir in cherries.
4. Spoon into bowls and serve while hot.

16)   Fluffy Quinoa Egg Muffin

Preparation time: 10 minutes

Cooking Time: 40 minutes

Serving: 12

Ingredients:
- Yellow onion chopped, one
- Quinoa, half cup
- Cooking spray
- Salt and Pepper, to taste
- Eggs, six
- Chopped red bell pepper, one
- Shredded mozzarella cheese, half cup
- Chopped baby spinach, one cup
- Garlic powder, half tsp.
- Paprika, half tsp.
- Milk, three tbsp.

Instructions:
1. Preheat oven to 350° and grease a 12-cup muffin tin with avocado or coconut oil cooking spray or coconut oil.
2. In a large nonstick skillet over medium heat, cook quinoa for six and eight minutes.
3. Drain on a paper towel-lined plate, then crumble.
4. Add onion and bell pepper to skillet and cook until soft approximately five minutes.
5. Add spinach and cook until wilted, two minutes more.

6. In a small bowl, whisk eggs, milk, paprika, and garlic powder and season with salt and pepper.
7. Fold in cooked vegetable mixture, quinoa, and mozzarella. Pour mixture into prepared muffin tin.
8. Bake until cooked through and golden for thirty minutes.
9. Your dish is ready to be served.

17)   Mushroom Scrambled Egg

Serving: 1

Preparation time: 5 minutes

Cook time: 5 minutes

Ingredients:

- 25g kale, chopped
- 1 tsp ground turmeric
- One egg
- 5g parsley finely chopped
- 1 tsp mild curry powder
- ½ sliced bird's eye chili
- sliced button mushrooms
- 1 tsp extra virgin olive oil

Instructions:

1. Make a paste of curry powder and turmeric by adding little water
2. Lightly warm the kale by steaming for 2 minutes
3. Fry the mushroom and bird's eye chili in a frying pan till they turn brown and soften on medium heat.
4. Now add spice paste and egg, cook on medium heat.
5. Add kale and cook on medium heat for one more minute.
6. Add parsley and mix it
7. It is ready to serve.

18)   Smoked Salmon Omelet

Serving: 1

Preparation time: 5 minutes

Cooking time: 4 minutes

Total time: 9 minutes

Ingredients:

- 100 g Smoked salmon, cut
- One tsp. extra virgin olive oil
- 2 Medium eggs
- 10 g chopped arugula leaves
- 1/2 tsp. capers
- One tsp. chopped parsley

Instructions:

1. Break the eggs into a bowl and whisk well. Include the salmon, tricks, rocket, and parsley.
2. Warm the olive oil in a non-stick skillet until hot yet not smoking. Include the egg blend and, utilizing a spatula or fish cut, move the blend around the container until it is even.
3. Decrease the heat on the stove and let the omelet cook through.
4. Slide the spatula around the edges and move up or overlay the omelet fifty-fifty to serve.
5. It is ready to serve.

19)   Shakshuka

Serving: 6

Preparation time: 15 minutes

Cook time: 20 minutes

Total Time: 35 minutes

Ingredients:

- One substantial red ringer pepper or broiled red chime pepper
- One huge onion, diced
- ¼ teaspoon fine ocean salt
- Two cloves garlic, squeezed or minced
- Six enormous eggs
- Two tablespoons tomato puree
- One to two tablespoons olive oil
- One teaspoon ground cumin
- ½ teaspoon smoked paprika

- ¼ teaspoon red pepper drops, decrease or overlook if touchy to flavor
- One enormous can squashed tomatoes, ideally fire-broiled
- ½ cup disintegrated feta
- Two tablespoons slashed new cilantro or level leaf parsley, and cilantro or parsley leaves for embellishing
- Newly ground dark pepper, to taste
- Dry bread or pita, for serving

Instructions:

1. Preheat the stove to 375 degrees Fahrenheit. Warm the oil in an enormous, broiler safe pan over the medium stove.
2. Once gleaming, add in the onion, ringer pepper, and salt. Cook, regularly mixing, until the onions are delicate and turning translucent, around four to six minutes.
3. Include the garlic, tomato puree, cumin, paprika, and red pepper pieces. Cook, blending continually, until quite fragrant, one to two minutes.
4. Pour in the squashed tomatoes with their juices and include the cilantro. Mix, and let the blend go to a stew. Diminish the stove heat as important to keep up a delicate stew, and cook for 5 minutes to give the flavors time to merge.
5. Switch off the stove. Taste it, and include salt and pepper as preferred. Utilize the rear of a spoon to make a well close to the border and split the egg legitimately into it. Delicately spoon a touch of the tomato blend over the whites to help contain the egg.

6. Rehash with the staying 4 to 5 eggs, contingent upon what number of you can fit. Sprinkle somewhat salt and pepper over the eggs.

7. Cautiously move the pan to the broiler and heat for 8 to 12 minutes, frequently checking once you arrive at 8 minutes. They're done when the egg whites are an obscure white, and the yolks have risen a piece however are still delicate. They should, at present, wiggle in the focuses when you shimmy the container.

8. Utilizing broiler gloves move the hot pan to a safe warmth surface like an oven. Top with the disintegrated feta, new cilantro leaves, and increasingly red pepper drops. However, you may prefer it. Serve in bowls with dry bread.

9. It is ready to serve.

20)   Blueberry Pancakes

Serving: 12

Preparation time: 10 minutes

Cook time: 10 minutes

Total time: 20 minutes

Ingredients:

- One egg
- One cup flour
- 3/4 cup milk
- Two tablespoons softened spread
- Two tablespoons white vinegar
- Two tablespoons sugar
- 1/2 teaspoon baking soda

- One teaspoon baking powder
- 1/2 teaspoon salt
- One cup blueberries
- more margarine for the container

Instructions:

1. Blend the milk and vinegar and let it sit for a moment or two.
2. Whisk the dry things together. Whisk the egg, milk, and softened spread into the dry ones until simply consolidated.
3. Heat a non-stick pan over a medium stove. Dissolve a little smear of margarine in the pan.
4. Pour around 1/3 cup of the mixture into the hot pan and spread it level like it will be entirely thick. Throw a couple of blueberries on top. Cook until you see little air pockets on top and the edges beginning to solidify. Flip and cook for another one to two minutes until they cooked through.
5. Present with margarine and maple syrup.
6. It is ready to eat.

21)   Black Bean Scrambled Eggs

Serving: 1

Preparation time: 10 minutes

Cook time: 15 minutes

Total time: 25 minutes

Ingredients:

- 1/3 medium avocado

- Two huge egg whites
- 1/2 tsp. olive oil
- One tbsp. salsa, no sugar included 1/2 cup dark beans, no sugar included whenever canned
- 1/4 medium onion, diced red onion is the most delicious

Instructions:

1. Sauté your onions in the oil in a non-stick pan.
2. Include your eggs and scramble or cook.
3. When eggs are close to cooked, mix in your beans and cook sufficiently long to warm them up.
4. Move to a plate and top with salsa and avocado.
5. It is ready to serve.

22)   Strawberry   Chocolate   chips   and Buckwheat Pancakes

Serving: 2

Preparation time: 5 minutes

Cook time: 30 minutes

Total time: 35 minutes

Ingredients:

- One huge egg
- One cup buckwheat flour
- One teaspoon baking powder
- Two tablespoons coconut sugar
- One tablespoon vanilla concentrate
- Two tablespoons additional virgin olive oil
- One teaspoon ground cinnamon
- 1/4 teaspoon fit salt
- 3/4 cup unsweetened cashew milk (or sans dairy milk of your decision)
- 1/2 cup hacked strawberries
- 1/4 cup dull chocolate chips
- Discretionary toppings:
- Ground flax seeds
- Maple syrup
- Chocolate Chips
- Diced Strawberries

Instructions:

1. Gently oil a pan and pre-heat on the medium stove.
2. In a medium-sized bowl, whisk together the flour, sugar, heating powder, cinnamon, and salt.
3. In a little bowl, whisk together the milk, oil, vanilla, and egg. Add the wet blend to the dry blend and mix until simply joined. Do not over blend. Overlay in the strawberries and chocolate chips.

4. Scoop out around 1/2 cup of the prepared mixture into the warmed skillet and spread it out into a 5-inch circle.
5. Cook for 4-5 minutes, or until the edges begin to cook and a couple of air pockets show up on top. Flip and cook for another 2-3 minutes.
6. Present with maple syrup and preferred garnishes.
7. It is ready to serve.

23)   Herb Omelet with Fita and Beans:

Serving: 2

Preparation time: 10 minutes

Cook time: 10 minutes

Total time: 20 minutes

Ingredients:

- 200g wide beans, podded weight
- Two little cubes of unsalted margarine
- Four medium eggs
- 75g vegan feta cheddar disintegrated or crumbled
- 1/2 pack tarragon leaves as it were
- 1/2 pack chives
- 1/2 pack level leaf parsley leaves as it were
- 1/2 lemon zest

Instructions:

1. Heat a pan of water to bubble and whiten the expansive beans for two minutes until simply delicate.

2. Deplete and revive under normal temperature running water.
3. Evacuate the external skin of the bean, to uncover the brilliant internal parts.
4. Split the eggs into a bowl and beat with a fork. Finely slash the herbs and speed into the eggs, alongside the vast majority of the lemon get-up-and-go and a lot of salt and newly ground dark pepper.
5. Warm a non-stick skillet over a medium-high stove. Include a little cube of spread at that point, while frothing, include in a large portion of the egg blend.
6. Utilize a spatula to move the egg around the container, letting it flood the spaces until it is nearly cooked.
7. Disperse a large portion of the cheddar and a large portion of the beans over the omelet.
8. Leave for 20-30 seconds, so the underside is completely set, and an exquisite brilliant earthy colored at that point overlay down the middle and slide onto a plate. Rehash for a subsequent omelet and serve quickly, dispersed with the held zest of lemon.
9. It is ready to serve.

24)   Date and Walnut Oatmeal

Serving: 1

Preparation time: 5 minutes

Cook time: 7 minutes

Total time: 12 minutes

Ingredients:

- 1/2 cups water

- 1/2 tsp. salt (discretionary)
- Two cups of oats
- 2/3 cup cleaved walnuts
- 2/3 cup cleaved dates

Instructions:

1. Heat the water and salt to the point of boiling.
2. Mix in the oats, walnuts, and dates.
3. Slow down the stove to medium.
4. Spread and cook for five minutes, mixing on more than one occasion.
5. Switch off the stove and let it cool down for two to three minutes before serving.
6. Present it with a sprinkle of earthy colored sugar or turbinado sugar and a sprinkle of milk or creamer.
7. Sprinkle over extra dates and walnuts whenever wanted.
8. It is ready to eat.

25)   Buckwheat Porridge

Serving: 2

Preparation time: 6 minutes

Cook time: 12 minutes

Total time: 18 minutes

Ingredients:

- Two cups of warm water
- One cup buckwheat, rinsed

Instructions:

1. Add buckwheat groats and water to a little pot to a medium high warmth. Heat to the point of boiling. Spread the pot with a top and put heat on low. Stew ten minutes, don't overcook. You can utilize a clock.
2. Following ten minutes, turn off warmth. Try not to open the cover, permit it to steam for an additional five minutes.
3. Cushion with a fork and serve. Top with fruits, almond milk, and a sprinkle of vanilla, a scramble of cinnamon, and a shower of maple syrup or nectar.
4. It is ready to serve.

4.2 Lunch Recipes

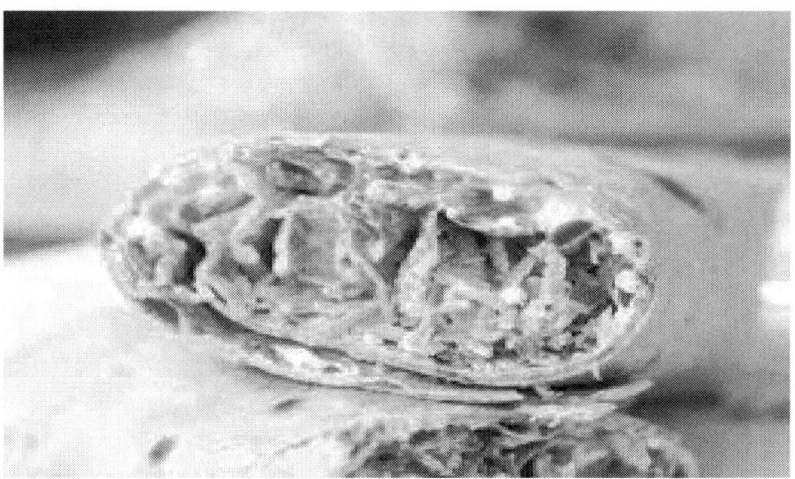

26)   Tangy Veggie Wrap

Preparation time: 6 minutes

Cook time: 12 minutes

Serving: 2

Ingredients:

- Sunflower seeds three tbsp.
- Carrots, two small
- Ginger one thumb
- Bell pepper half
- Red onion one
- Cottage cheese, half cup
- Sour cream, two tbsp.
- Lemon zest, one tsp.
- Mustard, three tsp.
- Wraps, two
- Spinach, half cup
- Salt and pepper to taste
- Bean sprouts, half cup

Instructions:

1. Roast the sunflower seeds in a pan without any oil until golden brown.
2. Peel and grate the carrots. Wash and dice the bell pepper.
3. Peel the onion and cut in thin rings.
4. Wash and drain the spinach.
5. Wash the bean sprouts with cold water and let them dry.
6. Peel the ginger and grate it into a bowl.
7. Add the cottage cheese, sour cream, lemon zest and mustard, and mix it well.
8. Spread the dressing mixture onto the wraps.
9. Lay out the spinach leaves on top.
10. Put the carrots, bell pepper, onions and bean sprouts in a wide line down the middle and sprinkle the roasted sunflower seeds on top.

11.   Season with a dash of salt and pepper and fold the wraps a little on both sides, then at the bottom and roll it as tightly as possible.
12.   Cut the wraps into halves and serve.

27)   King Prawn Stir Fry with Buckwheat Noodles

Serving: 1

Preparation time: 10 minutes

Cook time: 10 minutes

Total time: 20 minutes

Ingredients:

- 150 g shelled crude lord prawns, deveined
- Two tbsp. tamari
- Two tbsp. additional virgin olive oil
- 75 g soba (buckwheat) noodles
- One garlic clove, finely hacked
- One 10,000 foot bean stew, finely hacked
- One tsp. ginger, finely hacked
- 20 g red onion, cut
- 40 g celery
- 75 g green beans, diced
- Kale 50g, generally diced
- 100g chicken stock
- 5g lovage or celery leaves

Instructions:

1. Heat a skillet over a high stove, at that point, cook the prawns in one teaspoon of the tamari and one teaspoon of the oil for two to three minutes.
2. Move the prawns to a plate. Wipe the work out with kitchen paper, as you're going to utilize it once more.
3. Cook the noodles in bubbling water for five to eight minutes or as instructed on the bundle. Channel and put in a safe spot.
4. In the meantime, fry the garlic, stew and ginger, red onion, celery, beans, and kale in the rest of the oil over a medium-high warmth for two to three minutes.
5. Add the stock and bring to the bubble, at that point stew for a moment or two, until the vegetables are cooked yet crunchy.
6. Include the prawns, noodles, and lovage or celery leaves to the container, mix it thoroughly, and remove from the stove. It is ready to be eaten.

28)   Lemon Kale Salmon Pasta

Serving: 2

Nutritional Value: 620 calories

Preparation time: 10 minutes

Cook time: 15 minutes

Total time: 25 minutes

Ingredients:

- 4 oz wheat spaghetti (115 g)
- One boneless, skinless salmon, cubed
- Five tablespoons additional virgin olive oil
- Two cloves garlic, minced
- ¼ teaspoon red pepper chips
- 2 cups wavy kale (135 g), remove the ribs
- One lemon
- One tablespoon lemon juice
- legitimate salt, to taste
- ground dark pepper, to taste

Instructions:

1. Bubble salted water and cook the pasta for one moment, not exactly the time showed on the bundle. At the point when the pasta is done cooking, save ¼ cup (60 ml) of pasta water.
2. In the interim, heat two tablespoons of olive oil in a cast-iron skillet. Season cubed salmon with salt and pepper, add it to the skillet, and earthy colored it on each side. When cooked thoroughly around two to four minutes, remove from skillet and hold.
3. Cook three tablespoons of olive oil in a skillet and include garlic and red pepper drops. Cook until fragrant, around one minute.
4. Include kale, zests of lemon, lemon juice, salt, and saved pasta water. Cook until kale is delicate, around three minutes.
5. Include cooked salmon and pasta. Mix to cover and serve right away.

29)   Pot Prawns and Kale Curry

Serving: 4

Preparation time: 8 minutes

Cook time: 2 minutes

Total time: 10 minutes

Ingredients:

- Two cups chopped onions
- Two garlic cloves, minced or grated
- 1/2 inch ginger, minced or grated
- Two medium roman tomatoes, chopped, about 1 cup
- Four teaspoons coriander powder
- 1/2 to 1 teaspoon cayenne pepper powder, depending on your spice level
- 1/2 teaspoon turmeric powder
- One cinnamon stick
- Two cardamoms
- Two cloves
- 1/4 teaspoon fennel seeds
- Prawns, one pound
- Four stalks kale, ribs removed and coarsely chopped
- 1/2 cup coconut milk
- One cup of water
- 11/2 to 2 teaspoons salt, divided (or as per your taste)

Instructions:

1. Set your Pot to sauté, include vegetable oil when hot. Include every entire flavor and let toast for a few moments.
2. Include all spices, sauté until onions turn translucent, around four minutes.
3. Sauté until tomatoes are soft, flavors are toasted well, and it starts to turn gleaming. Ensure you sauté like clockwork at this stage, causing sure that it doesn't to consume at the base.
4. Set manual for five minutes, ensuring the valve is set at fixing position.
5. Following five minutes, let your pot be in warm mode for two to four minutes. Go valve to vent and discharge the pressure.
6. Check for salt and present with your preferred side dish or cool and pack into boxes for use afterwards.

30)   Baked Tofu Wraps

Serving: 6

Nutritional Value: 360 calories

Preparation time: 15 minutes

Cook time: 30 minutes

Total time: 45 minutes

Ingredients:

- One square of extra-firm tofu depleted and squeezed.
- Six tablespoons corn-starch

- ⅓ cup unsweetened almond milk or milk of decision
- One cup oats
- Two tablespoon olive or avocado oil
- ½ teaspoon paprika
- One teaspoon dried oregano
- ½ teaspoon salt
- ¼ teaspoon dark pepper
- Six entire wheat wraps or tortillas
- Discretionary sauces and toppings
- 5g lovage or celery leaves

Instructions:

1. Preheat broiler to 425 Fahrenheit and line an enormous preparing sheet with material paper. Put in a safe spot.
2. Cut squeezed tofu into 24 little square shapes (does not need to be definite, fundamentally simply make them reduced down). Spot tofu shapes in a bowl.
3. Next, join in the oats, oil, paprika, oregano, salt, and pepper in a shallow bowl until all around consolidated.
4. Set up your tofu toward the start, trailed by corn starch in a shallow bowl, at that point a bowl of almond milk, lastly a shallow bowl with the breadcrumb blend. Toward the stopping point ought to be the material lined preparing sheet.
5. Coat tofu pieces by dunking each piece into the corn starch, at that point the almond milk, and afterward the breadcrumb blend (once more, make a point to cover all the sides). Spot covered tofu on the readied heating sheet and rehash with extra tofu. Make sure to keep covered tofu pieces

at any rate one to two inches separated on the preparing sheet.

6. Prepare tofu for twenty five minutes, flip, and cook another five to ten minutes.
7. Remove from the stove. Alternatively, you can hurl your tofu in BBQ sauce, and afterward gather your wraps.
8. They are ready to eat.

31)   Tofu and Kale Pesto Sandwich

Serving: 2

Preparation time: 15 minutes

Cook time: 5 minutes

Total time: 20 minutes

Ingredients:

- Smoked tofu, seven ounce
- Olive oil, 5-6 tbsp.
- Walnuts, half cup
- Yeast, one tsp.
- Italian herb mix, two tsp.
- Kale, one cup
- Minced garlic, one
- ½ teaspoon salt
- ¼ teaspoon dark pepper
- Zucchini, one
- Carrot, one
- Wheat buns, two

- Lettuce

Instructions:

1. First make the kale pesto.
2. Put all ingredients into a blender or food processor and blend until smooth.
3. Cut the tofu into thin strips.
4. In a medium pan, heat some olive oil and stir-fry the tofu for about two minutes on each side until it is brown and crispy.
5. If you want you can also add about half a teaspoon of soy sauce. Once the tofu is done, put it aside.
6. Heat some more olive oil and cook the zucchini slices for another three minutes. Season with salt, pepper, and Italian spices (such as oregano, basil, rosemary, thyme).
7. Cut the sandwiches in half and generously coat both sides with kale pesto.
8. Add the lettuce, the tofu, the carrots, and the grilled zucchini.

32)   Sautéed Kale

Serving: 4

Nutritional Value: 98 calories

Preparation time: 5 minutes

Cook time: 20 minutes

Total time: 25 minutes

Ingredients:

- One tablespoon in addition to one teaspoon extra-virgin olive oil for later use

- 1/2 pounds kale, ribs evacuated, coarsely cleaved
- ½ cup of water
- Two cloves garlic, minced
- ¼ teaspoon squashed red pepper
- Two to three teaspoons sherry vinegar or red-wine vinegar
- ¼ teaspoon salt

Instructions:
1. Warm one tablespoon oil in a broiler over a medium stove.
2. Include kale and cook, hurling with two huge spoons, until brilliant green, around one moment.
3. Include water; lessen warmth to medium-low, spread and cook, mixing at times, until the kale is delicate, about fifteen minutes.
4. Push kale aside, include the staying one teaspoon oil to the unfilled side and cooking garlic, and squash red pepper in it until it is fragrant, Switch off from the stove and hurl together. Mix in vinegar to taste and salt.
5. It is ready to serve.

33) Shrimp Butternut Squash and Date Tagine

Serving: 4

Nutritional Value: 244 calories

Preparation time: 15 minutes

Cook time: 1 hour and 15 minutes

Total time: 1 hour and 30 minutes

Ingredients:

- Two tablespoons olive oil
- One red onion, cut
- 2cm ginger, ground
- Two garlic cloves, ground or squashed
- One teaspoon bean stew drops (or to taste)
- Two teaspoons cumin seeds
- One cinnamon stick
- Two teaspoons ground turmeric
- 800g Shrimps
- ½ teaspoon salt
- 100g Medjool dates, hollowed and slashed
- 400g tin slashed tomatoes, in addition to a large portion of a jar of water
- 500g butternut squash cut into 1cm shapes
- 400g tin chickpeas, depleted
- Two tablespoons new coriander (in addition to this extra for decorations in the end)
- Buckwheat, couscous, flatbreads or rice to serve

Instructions:

1. Preheat your broiler to 140 Celsius.
2. Drizzle around two tablespoons of olive oil into an enormous ovenproof pot or cast iron goulash dish. Add in the previously diced onion and cook on a delicate heat, with the cover on, for around 5 minutes, until the onions are mellowed yet not earthy colored.
3. Add the ground garlic and ginger, bean stew, cumin, cinnamon, and turmeric. Mix well and cook for progressively one minute with the top off. Include a sprinkle of water in the event that it gets excessively dry.
4. Next include the shrimps. Mix well to cover the meat in the onions and flavors and afterward include the salt, slashed dates, and tomatoes, in addition to about a large portion of a container of water (100-200ml).
5. Bring the tagine to bubble and afterward put the top on and put in your preheated broiler for 1 hour and 15 minutes.
6. Thirty minutes before the finishing of the cooking time, include the cleaved butternut squash and chickpeas. Mix everything together, set the top back on, and come back to the broiler for the last 30 minutes of cooking.
7. When the tagine is prepared, quickly remove from the stove and mix through the cleaved coriander. Present with buckwheat, couscous, flatbreads, or basmati rice.
8. It is ready to be served.

34)   Prawn Arabiata

Serving: 1

Nutritional Value: 420 calories

Preparation time: 40 minutes

Cook time: 30 minutes

Total time: 1 hour and 10 minutes

Ingredients:
- 125-150 g Raw or cooked prawns
- 65 g Buckwheat pasta
- One tbsp Extra virgin olive oil

For the sauce:
- One tsp Dried blended herbs
- 40 g Red onion, finely cleaved
- 30 g Celery, finely cleaved
- One Bird's eye bean stew, finely cleaved
- One tsp Extra virgin olive oil
- One Garlic clove, finely cleaved
- One tbsp Chopped parsley
- Two tbsp White wine (discretionary)
- 400 g Tinned cleaved tomatoes

Instructions:
1. Fry the onion, garlic, celery, and bean stew and dried herbs in the oil over a medium-low stove for one to two minutes.
2. Turn the warmth up to medium, include the wine, and cook for one moment. Include the tomatoes and leave the sauce to stew over medium-low heat for 20–30 minutes, until it has a decent creamy consistency.
3. If you feel the sauce is getting too thick, essentially include a little water.

4. While the sauce is cooking, Take a skillet of water and boil it till bubbles appear and cook the pasta as indicated on the parcel.
5. At the point when prepared exactly as you would prefer, channel, hurl with the olive oil and keep in the skillet until required.
6. If you are utilizing crude prawns, add them to the sauce and cook for a further three to four minutes until they have turned pink and murky, include the parsley and serve.
7. In the event that you are utilizing cooked prawns, include them with the parsley, boil the sauce till bubbles appear and serve.
8. Add the cooked pasta to the sauce, blend completely yet tenderly and serve.

35)   Baked Turmeric Salmon

Serving: 1

Nutritional Value: 358 calories

Preparation time: 15 minutes

Cook time: 10 minutes

Total time: 25 minutes

Ingredients:

- 125-150 g Skinned Salmon
- 1 tsp Extra virgin olive oil
- 1 tsp ground turmeric
- 1/4 Juice of a lemon

For celery:

- 1 tsp Extra virgin olive oil
- 40 g Red onion, finely diced
- 60 g Tinned green lentils
- 1 Garlic clove, finely diced
- 1 cm fresh ginger, finely diced
- 1 Bire's eye stew, finely crushed
- 150 g Celery cut into 2cm lengths
- 1 tsp Mild curry powder
- 130 g Tomato, cut into eight pieces
- 100 ml Chicken or vegetable stock
- 1 tbsp Chopped parsley

Instructions:

1. Warm the stove
2. Start with preparing the hot celery. Warm a skillet over medium-low warmth, including the olive oil, at that point the onion, garlic, ginger, stew, and celery. Fry tenderly for 2–3 minutes or until mellowed yet not shaded. At that point, include the curry powder and cook for a further moment.
3. Add the tomatoes, then the stock and lentils, and stew delicately for 10 minutes. You might need to increment or reduction the cooking time contingent upon how crunchy you like your celery.
4. Meanwhile, blend the turmeric, oil, and lemon squeeze and rub over the salmon. Place on a heating plate and cook for ten minutes.
5. To complete, mix the parsley through the celery and present it with the salmon.
6. Your dish is ready to serve.

36)   Shrimp Coronation Salad

Serving: 1

Nutritional Value: 105 calories

Preparation time: 5 minutes

Cook time: 0 minutes

Total time: 5 minutes

Ingredients:

- 75 g Natural yogurt
- One Bird's eye stew
- 1/2 tsp Mild curry powder
- 100 g Cooked shrimps
- Juice of 1/4 of a lemon
- One tsp Coriander, finely chopped
- One tsp ground turmeric
- 20 g Red onion, diced
- Walnut parts, finely diced
- 40 g Rocket, to serve
- One Medjool date, finely diced

Instructions:

1. Blend the yogurt, lemon juice, coriander, and flavors together in a bowl.
2. Include all the rest of the things and serve on a bed of the arugula leaves.
3. Eat well and stay healthy and fresh.

37) Spicy Chickpea Stew with Baked Potatoes

Serving: 4

Nutritional Value: 358 calories

Preparation time: 10 minutes

Cook time: 1 hour

Total time: 1 hour and 10 minutes

Ingredients:

- Two red onions, finely cleaved
- 4-6 heating potatoes, pricked everywhere
- 2 x 400g tins cleaved tomatoes
- 2cm ginger, ground
- Two tablespoons olive oil
- cloves garlic, ground or squashed
- ½ - 2 teaspoons bean stew chips (contingent upon how hot you like things)
- Two yellow peppers (or whatever shading you prefer), cleaved into bite-size pieces
- Two tablespoons turmeric
- Two tablespoons cumin seeds
- Sprinkle of water
- Two tablespoons unsweetened cocoa powder (or cacao)
- 2 x 400g tins chickpeas
- Two tablespoons parsley in addition to extra for embellish
- A side plate of mixed greens, discretionary

- Salt and pepper to taste, discretionary

Instructions:

1. Preheat the stove to 200C. In the interim, you can set up the entirety of your mixings.
2. When the broiler is hot enough, placed your heating potatoes in the stove and cook for 1 hour or until they are done how you like them.
3. Once the potatoes are in the stove, place the olive oil and slashed red onion in an enormous wide pan and cook tenderly, with the cover on for five minutes, until the onions are delicate yet not earthy colored.
4. Remove the cover and include the garlic, ginger, cumin, and bean stew. Cook for a further moment on a low, warm stove, at that point, include the turmeric and an exceptionally little sprinkle of water and cook for one more moment, taking consideration not to let the dish get excessively dry.
5. Next, include the tomatoes, cocoa powder, chickpeas (counting the chickpea water), and yellow pepper. Bring to a bubble, at that point, stew on low warmth for 45 minutes until the sauce is thick and unctuous. The stew ought to be done at generally a similar time as the potatoes.
6. Finally, mix in the two tablespoons of parsley and some salt and pepper in the event that you wish it to be spicy, and serve the stew on the prepared potatoes, maybe with a basic side plate of mixed greens.
7. Enjoy your meal.

38)   Kale   and   Red   Onion   Dhal   with Buckwheat

Serving: 4

Nutritional Value: 420 calories

Preparation time: 5 minutes

Cook time: 25 minutes

Total time: 30 minutes

Ingredients:

- One tablespoon olive oil
- One little red onion, cut
- 160g buckwheat (or earthy colored rice)
- 400ml coconut milk
- Two garlic cloves, ground or squashed
- Two cm ginger, ground
- 200ml water
- One birds-eye bean stew, deseeded and finely diced (more if you like things hot)
- Two teaspoons turmeric
- Two teaspoons garam masala
- 160g red lentils
- 100g kale (or spinach would be an extraordinary other option)

Instructions:

1. Put the olive oil in an enormous, profound pan and include the cut onion. Cook on a low warmth, with the top on for five minutes until mellowed.
2. Add the garlic, ginger and bean stew and cook for 1 minute.
3. Add the turmeric, garam masala, and a sprinkle of water and cook for one minute.

4. Add the red lentils, coconut milk, and 200ml water.
5. Mix everything together completely and cook for 20 minutes over a delicately heat with the cover on. Mix once in a while and include somewhat more water if the dhal begins to stick.
6. After 20 minutes, including the kale, mix all together and supplant the top, cook for a further 5 minutes.
7. About 15 minutes before the curry is prepared, place the buckwheat in a medium pan, and include a lot of bubbling water. Take the water back to the bubble and cook for ten minutes. Channel the buckwheat in a strainer and present with the dhal.
8. Your dish is ready to be served.

39)   Choc Chip Granola

Serving: 8

Nutritional Value: 244 calories

Preparation time: 10 minutes

Cook time: 20 minutes

Total time: 30 minutes

Ingredients:

- 200g normal sized oats
- 50g walnuts, generally cleaved
- Two tbsp light olive oil
- 20g margarine
- One tbsp brown colored sugar
- Two tbsp rice malt syrup

- 60g dim chocolate chips

Instructions:

1. Preheat the broiler to 160°C. Line a huge heating plate with a silicone sheet or preparing material.
2. Combine the oats and walnuts in an enormous bowl. In a little non-stick container, delicately heat the olive oil, spread, earthy colored sugar, and rice malt syrup until the margarine has liquefied and the sugar and syrup have broken down.
3. Try not to permit to bubble. Pour the syrup over the oats and mix completely until the oats are completely secured.
4. Distribute the granola over the heating plate, spreading directly into the corners.
5. Leave clusters of blend with separating instead of an even spread. Prepare in the stove for 20 minutes until just touched brilliant earthy colored at the edges.
6. Remove from the broiler and leave to cool on the plate totally.
7. When cool, separate the greater knots on the plate with your fingers and afterward blend in the chocolate chips.
8. Scoop or empty the granola into an impenetrable tub or container.
9. The granola will save for fourteen days so you can make it in bulk.

40)   Parmesan Chicken and Kale

Serving: 4

Nutritional Value: 402 calories

Preparation time: 10 minutes

Cook time: 19 minutes

Total time: 29 minutes

Ingredients:

- Two tablespoons olive oil
- 1/2 pound scampi
- Fit salt
- Newly ground dark pepper
- One medium yellow onion, diced
- Two cloves garlic, minced
- Squeeze red pepper drops
- One enormous bundle level leaf kale (around 12 ounces), stems evacuated and leaves coarsely cut
- 1/2 cup dry white wine
- 1/2 cup ground Parmesan cheddar
- One tablespoon newly made lemon juice

Instructions:

1. Warm the oil in a huge skillet keep the stove on medium heat until sparkling. Include the scampi into it, season with salt and pepper, and sauté until cooked thoroughly for five to seven minutes. Move the scampi to a plate and spread it with some wrap to keep warm.
2. Include the onion, garlic, and pepper pieces to the skillet. Sauté until the onions are beginning to mollify, around two minutes. Mix in the kale, wine, and a touch of salt. Spread and cook for around five minutes, mixing every so often, until the kale is simply delicate.
3. Add the scampi and any amassed juices to the skillet. Include the Parmesan and lemon squeeze and mix it thoroughly. Taste and season with increasingly salt and pepper according to your liking.
4. It is ready to be served.

41)   Caesar Salad

Preparation Time: 12 minutes

Cooking Time: 12 minutes

Serving: 4

Ingredients:

- Garlic pepper, one tsp.
- Garlic minced and mashed, one clove
- Romaine lettuce, chopped
- Fresh shredded Asiago cheese
- Toasted croutons.
- Hellman's mayonnaise, half cup
- Finely grated parmesan cheese, half cup

- Buttermilk, 1/4 cup
- Sweet and sour dressing, half cup
- Dry Ranch dressing mix, two tsp.

Instructions:

1. Combine the ingredients for the dressing.
2. Add dressing to the lettuce, to taste.
3. Mix well and refrigerate.
4. Serve topped with shredded Asiago cheese and toasted croutons.

42)   Caribbean Salad with Grilled Prawns

Preparation time: 10 minutes

Cooking Time: 10 minutes

Serving: 2

Ingredients:

- Teriyaki Sauce, half cup
- Tortilla chips
- Iceberg lettuce, half cup
- Pineapple chunks, half cup
- Cabbage, half cup
- Olive oil, half cup
- Jalapeno peppers three tbsp.
- Onion, diced, half cup
- Cilantro, two bunches
- Tomatoes, half cup
- Honey, two tbsp.
- Sugar, one tsp.

- Sesame oil, one tsp.
- Lime juice, one tsp.
- Wine vinegar, one and a half tsp.
- Grilled prawns
- Apple cider vinegar, one tbsp.

Instructions:

1. Marinate the chicken in the teriyaki for at least two hours.
2. Use a plastic bag. Put in fridge.
3. Preheat outdoor or indoor grill.
4. Grill the prawns for 4-5 mins.
5. Toss the lettuces and cabbage together and divide into 2 large serving size salad bowls.
6. Divide the pineapple and sprinkle on salads.
7. Break tortilla chips into large chunks and sprinkle on salads.
8. Slice the grilled prawns and divide among bowls.
9. Pour the dressing into two small bowls and serve with the salads.

43)   Caribbean Salad with Shrimps

Preparation time: 10 minutes

Cooking Time: 10 minutes

Serving: 2

Ingredients:

- Teriyaki Sauce, half cup
- Tortilla chips
- Iceberg lettuce, half cup
- Pineapple chunks, half cup
- Cabbage, half cup
- Olive oil, half cup
- Jalapeno peppers three tbsp.

- Onion, diced, half cup
- Cilantro, two bunches
- Tomatoes, half cup
- Honey, two tbsp.
- Sugar, one tsp.
- Sesame oil, one tsp.
- Lime juice, one tsp.
- Wine vinegar, one and a half tsp.
- Shrimps
- Apple cider vinegar, one tbsp.

Instructions:

1. Marinate the shrimps in the teriyaki for at least two hours.
2. Use a plastic bag. Put in fridge.
3. Preheat outdoor or indoor grill.
4. Grill the shrimps for 4-5 mins.
5. Toss the lettuces and cabbage together and divide into 2 large serving size salad bowls.
6. Divide the pineapple and sprinkle on salads.
7. Break tortilla chips into large chunks and sprinkle on salads.
8. Place the grilled shrimps and divide among bowls.
9. Pour the dressing into two small bowls and serve with the salads.

44)   Spicy Shrimp Tacos

Preparation time: 10 minutes

Cooking Time: 10 minutes

Serving: 3

Ingredients:

- Tortilla, three
- Shrimps, six

- Iceberg lettuce, half cup
- Cabbage, half cup
- Avocado, two slices
- Chili powder, a pinch
- Mayonnaise, three tbsp.
- Onion, diced, half cup
- Thai sweet chili sauce, one tbsp.
- Siracha, one tbsp.

Instructions:

1. Heat a grill pan over medium heat and wipe surface with olive oil.
2. Season the shrimp with the salt, pepper and chili powder, and then grill for three to five minutes until done.
3. In a small bowl, mix together the mayo, sweet chili sauce and siracha together.
4. Warm the tortillas and place half of the cabbage on each tortilla.
5. Drizzle half the sauce over each taco.
6. Top with shrimp & garnish with avocado.
7. Serve immediately.

45)   Zuppa Toscana Soup

Preparation time: 10 minutes

Cooking Time: 35 minutes

Serving: 4

Ingredients:

- Water, two cups
- Minced garlic, one tbsp.
- Butter, four tbsp.
- Heavy cream, two cups
- Chopped kale, two cups
- Onion, half
- Ground fish sausage, half pound
- Salt and pepper to taste
- Potatoes, half cup

Instructions:

1. Mix all the ingredients together in a large pot.
2. Cook for 35 minutes and then serve hot.

46)   Herb Grilled Salmon

Preparation time: 10 minutes

Cooking Time: 15 minutes

Serving: 4

Ingredients:

- Salmon fillet, two pounds
- Lemon, two, cut in halves

- Butter, half cup
- Italian seasoning, two tbsp.
- Steamed rice, two cups
- Parsley, half cup
- Minced garlic, one tsp.
- Salt and pepper to taste

Instructions:

1. Season the salmon with salt, pepper, and Italian Seasoning, rubbing them well on both sides.
2. Allow the salmon to briefly marinade on a slotted tray, at least for fifteen minutes.
3. Place the salmon on the grill skin side down and brush with oil on both sides. You may also use cooking spray.
4. Cook the salmon, flipping it regularly until it is cooked through.
5. Bring your butter out from the chiller & slice a half cm thick ring. Return any excess back to the chiller, and discard any paper wrapping of the cut portion.
6. Once the salmon is cooked, serve it with rice, lemon wedges, your garlic butter on top, and your choice of vegetables.

47)   Chicken Scampi

Preparation time: 10 minutes

Cooking Time: 20 minutes

Serving: 4

Ingredients:

- Olive oil, two tbsp.
- Minced garlic, one and a half tsp.

- Flour, one tbsp.
- Heavy cream, two cups
- Onion, half cup
- Scampi, half pound
- Salt and pepper to taste
- Parmesan cheese, half cup
- Mix bell peppers, sliced
- Angel hair, twelve ounces

Instructions:

1. Season scampi.
2. Place flour in a shallow dish and season with one tsp seasoned salt.
3. Dredge scampi in flour.
4. Heat one tbsp. olive oil in large skillet.
5. Place scampi in skillet and cook over medium high heat for four minutes. Flip and cook for three to four more minutes. Remove to a plate.
6. Add one tbsp. oil to skillet.
7. Add peppers and onions. Season with salt and pepper. Sauté for about five minutes.
8. Add garlic and sauté for a few more minutes.
9. Add cream, milk, and parmesan. Bring to a simmer.
10. Add scampi and let simmer for five minutes.
11. Your dish is ready to be served.

48)   Shrimp Alfredo

Preparation time: 10 minutes

Cooking Time: 20 minutes

Serving: 4

Ingredients:

- Olive oil, two tbsp.
- Minced garlic, one and a half tsp.
- Flour, one tbsp.
- Butter, four tbsp.
- Heavy cream, two cups
- Parsley, half cup
- Shrimp, half pound
- Salt and pepper to taste
- Parmesan cheese, half cup
- Pasta, one cup

Instructions:

1. Add oil into a pan and then garlic.
2. Add butter, cream and flour and mix until uniform mixture is formed.
3. Add shrimps and cook and then add pasta.
4. Serve in a bowl with parsley and parmesan cheese on top.

49) Hickory Bourbon Salmon

Preparation time: 20 minutes

Cooking Time: 20 minutes

Serving: 3

Ingredients:

- Bourbon, one cup
- Soy sauce, two tbsp.
- Chopped chives, one tsp.
- Brown sugar, two tbsp.
- Salt and pepper to taste
- Salmon fillet, one pound
- Olive oil, two tbsp.

- Garlic powder, half tsp.

Instructions:

1. Combine pineapple juice, brown sugar, bourbon, soy sauce, pepper and garlic powder in a bowl.
2. Stir to dissolve sugar. Add the oil.
3. Remove skin and bones from salmon fillets.
4. Put fillets in baking dish and pour marinade over and let sit in the fridge for one hour or longer.
5. The longer it can sit the more the marinade seeps into the fillets.
6. Cook the salmon filets on the grill or on the stove top on medium heat.
7. Brush the extra marinade over the fillets as they are cooking.
8. Arrange the fillets on a plate and sprinkle with the chopped chives.

50)   New Orleans

Preparation time: 10 minutes

Cooking Time: 15 minutes

Serving: 4

Ingredients:

- Tilapa fillet, two pounds
- Shrimp, one pound
- Butter, four tbsp.
- Creole seasoning, two tbsp.
- Alfredo sauce, half cup
- Olive oil, three tbsp.
- Minced garlic, one tsp.
- Salt and pepper to taste

Instructions:

1. Preheat oven to 425 degree.
2. Wash and dry tilapia fillets, spread with olive oil and creole seasoning, to your taste.
3. Place in well oiled baking pan, bake for ten minutes, until just white.
4. While fish is baking, warm Alfredo in a small saucepan.
5. In a fry pan, melt three tbsp. butter, add minced garlic and cleaned, prepared shrimp sauté for about five minutes.
6. When fish is ready, remove pan from oven.
7. Carefully remove fillets to plates, top with cooked shrimp and Alfredo sauce.

4.3 Dinner Recipes

51)   Kale, Edamame and Tofu Curry

Serving: 4

Nutritional Value: 342 calories

Preparation time: 10 minutes

Cook time: 35 minutes

Total time: 45 minutes

Ingredients:

- 200g kale leaves stalks evacuated and torn
- One tbsp rapeseed oil
- Two cloves garlic stripped and ground
- One red bean stew, deseeded and meagerly cut
- One enormous onion, diced
- One enormous thumb size (7cm) ginger, removed and ground
- 1/2 tsp ground turmeric
- One tsp paprika
- 1/2 tsp ground cumin
- 1/4 tsp cayenne pepper
- 1 tsp salt
- 250g dried red lentils
- 50g solidified soy edamame beans
- 200g firm tofu slashed into solid shapes
- One liter bubbling water
- Two tomatoes, generally slashed
- Juice of 1 lime

Instructions:

1. Put the oil in an overwhelming bottomed container over a low-medium stove. Include the onion and cook for 5 minutes before including the garlic, ginger and bean stew and cooking for a further 2 minutes. Include the turmeric, cayenne, paprika, cumin, and salt. Mix thoroughly before including the red lentils and mixing once more.
2. Pour in the bubbling water and make a generous stew by boiling for ten minutes, at that point decrease the warmth of the stove and cook for a further 20-30 minutes until the curry has a thick consistency.
3. Add the soya beans, tofu, and tomatoes and cook for a further five minutes. Include the lime juice and kale leaves and cook until the kale is simply delicate.
4. Your dish is ready to be served.

52)   Grilled Salmon

Preparation time: 10 minutes

Cooking Time: 15 minutes

Serving: 4

Ingredients:

- Salmon fillet, two pounds
- Butter, half cup
- Italian seasoning, two tbsp.
- Steamed rice, two cups
- Parsley, half cup
- Minced garlic, one tsp.
- Salt and pepper to taste

Instructions:

1. Season the salmon with salt, pepper, and Italian seasoning, rubbing them well on both sides.
2. Allow the salmon to briefly marinade on a slotted tray, at least for fifteen minutes.
3. Place the salmon on the grill skin side down and brush with oil on both sides. You may also use cooking spray.
4. Cook the salmon, flipping it regularly until it is cooked through.
5. Bring your butter out from the chiller & slice a half cm thick ring.
6. Once the salmon is cooked, serve it with rice, your garlic butter on top, and your choice of vegetables.

53) Parmesan Shrimp Pasta

Preparation time: 10 minutes

Cooking Time: 20 minutes

Serving: 4

Ingredients:

- Olive oil, two tbsp.
- Minced garlic, one and a half tsp.
- Flour, one tbsp.
- Butter, four tbsp.
- Heavy cream, two cups
- Parsley, half cup
- Shrimp, half pound
- Salt and pepper to taste
- Parmesan cheese, half cup
- Pasta, one cup

Instructions:

1. Add oil into a pan and then garlic.
2. Add butter, cream and flour and mix until uniform mixture is formed.
3. Add shrimps and cook and then add pasta.
4. Serve in a bowl with parsley and parmesan cheese on top.

54)   Ranch Pasta

Preparation time: 10 minutes

Cooking Time: 20 minutes

Serving: 2

Ingredients:

- Olive oil, two tbsp.
- Mayonnaise, one tbsp.
- Frozen peas, four tbsp.
- Buttermilk, one cup
- Ranch dressing, half cup
- Salt and pepper to taste
- Ricotta cheese, half cup
- Pasta, one cup

Instructions:

1. Bring a pot of water to a boil and cook pasta.
2. Drain into a colander and rinse with cold water until pasta is cool.
3. Set pasta aside and allow to dry for about thirty minutes.
4. While pasta is cooking, combine mayonnaise, buttermilk, ranch dressing mix, and season salt in a large bowl and mix until combined.
5. Add in frozen peas and stir. The peas will thaw a bit during mixing and will finish thawing while pasta cools.
6. Add dry rotini and mix until well blended.
7. Your pasta is ready to be served.

55) Miso Marinated Cod with Stir-Fried Greens:

Serving: 1

Nutritional Value: 450 calories

Preparation time: 12 minutes

Cook time: 20 minutes

Total time: 22 minutes

Ingredients:

- 50g kale, generally cut
- One garlic clove, finely diced
- One tbsp mirin
- 200g skinless cod filet
- One tbsp additional virgin olive oil
- 20g miso 60g green beans
- 40g celery, cut
- 20g red onion, cut
- One tsp finely crushed new ginger
- One tsp ground turmeric
- One tsp sesame seeds
- 5g parsley, usually cut
- 30g buckwheat
- One tbsp tamari

Instructions:

1. Warm the stove to 220°C.
2. Blend the miso, mirin, and one teaspoon of the oil. Rub everywhere throughout the cod and leave to marinate for 30 minutes. Prepare the cod for 10 minutes.
3. In the interim, heat a huge griddle or wok with the rest of the oil. Include the onion and sautéed food for a couple of moments. At that point include the celery, garlic, stew, ginger, green beans, and kale. Hurl and fry until the kale is delicate and cooked through. You may need to add a little water to the skillet to help the cooking procedure.
4. Cook the buckwheat as indicated by the parcel guidelines with the turmeric for 3 minutes.
5. Include the sesame seeds, parsley, and tamari to the sautéed food and present with the greens and fish.
6. Your dish is ready to be served.

56)   Potato Soup

Preparation time: 12 minutes

Cooking Time: 30 minutes

Serving: 6

Ingredients:

- Cornstarch, two tbsp.
- Potato, two
- Green Onions, chopped, three
- Ginger, grated, half tsp.
- Water, two tbsp.
- Chicken broth, four cups
- Soy Sauce, one tbsp.

Instructions:

1. Mix all the ingredients together, and boil it for about thirty minutes.
2. Add the cornstarch in the end, and mix properly.
3. Your soup is ready to be served.

57)   Toowoomba Pasta Recipe

Preparation Time: 20 minutes

Cooking Time: 30 minutes

Serving: 4

Ingredients:

- Parmesan cheese, half cup
- Fettuccini, one box
- Cornstarch, one tbsp.
- Garlic powder
- Ketchup, two tbsp.
- Olive oil, one tbsp.
- Cream, one tbsp.
- Shrimps, half pound
- Small onion, diced, one
- Butter, two tbsp.
- Large mushrooms, sliced, four
- Salt and pepper, to taste

Instructions:

1. Cook fettuccine as directed.
2. Melt butter in a large skillet.
3. Whisk in cream, ketchup and spices.
4. Bring to a boil.
5. Continue to simmer and reduce while you continue with the rest of the recipe, stirring occasionally with a wire whisk.
6. Sauté mushrooms in a separate small skillet over medium to low heat, in olive oil until soft.
7. Add mushrooms to simmering sauce.
8. Cook shrimp in the small skillet in olive oil just until pink and add to sauce.
9. Simmer for about five minutes adding green onions for the last two minutes or so.
10. In a large bowl, toss shrimp mixture with cooked and drained fettuccine and serve immediately, topping with finely shredded fresh parmesan cheese.
11. Your dish is ready.

58)   Seafood Stuffed Mushrooms

Preparation time: 10 minutes

Cooking Time: 25 minutes

Serving: 6

Ingredients:

- Oil, one quart
- Garlic powder, half tsp.
- Eggs, two
- Milk, one cup
- Crab meat, half pound
- Wheat flour, half cup
- Fresh mushrooms, one pound
- Cheddar cheese, half cup

- Salt, half tsp.
- Oyster crackers, two cups
- Red bell peppers, two
- Onions, one
- Celery, a quarter cup

Instructions:

1. Preheat oven to 400 degrees.
2. Wash mushrooms and remove stems.
3. Set caps aside, and chop half of the stems.
4. Sauté chopped mushroom stems, celery, onion and pepper in butter for two minutes.
5. Transfer to a plate and cool in refrigerator.
6. Combine sautéed vegetables and all other ingredients and mix well.
7. Place mushroom caps in a sprayed or buttered baking pan stem side up.
8. Spoon one tsp stuffing into each mushroom cap.
9. Cover with a piece of sliced cheese.
10. Bake for fifteen minutes until cheese is lightly brown.

59) Lobster Bisque

Preparation time: 10 minutes

Cooking Time: 30 minutes

Serving: 4

Ingredients:

- Water, six cups
- Fish stock, two cups
- Green Onions, chopped, three
- Carrot, one cup
- Celery, one cup
- Lobsters, one pound
- Ginger, grated, half tsp.
- White wine, two tbsp.
- Potato, two
- Cream, one cup
- Cognac, a quarter cup
- Tomatoes, one and a half cup
- Paprika and thyme, one tbsp.
- All-purpose flour, one cup

Instructions:

1. Place the water, the white wine and the fish stock into a wide, deep pot, and bring to a boil on high heat.
2. Place lobsters, topside down, in the broth.
3. Reduce heat to medium and cook covered for approximately six minutes.
4. Remove lobsters from broth and put them to the side.
5. When the lobsters are cool enough to handle, begin removing the meat from the shell, dicing the pieces into half inch cubes.
6. Store the lobster meat in the refrigerator until later.
7. Place the lobster shells back into the broth, reduce heat to a simmer and cook uncovered for twenty minutes.
8. Strain the broth through a sieve into a container and store in the refrigerator until later.
9. Discard the lobster shells.

10. Put your pot back on the stove under medium heat.
11. Pour in the melted butter.
12. Once the butter is heated up, add the onions, carrots, celery and garlic.
13. Add the cognac and cook until the alcohol has evaporated.
14. Mix in the flour, stirring with a heavy gauge spatula or spoon until the mixture is blond in color and has a buttery aroma.
15. Mix the diced tomatoes, paprika, thyme and ground pepper with the cold broth from the refrigerator.
16. Then, pour the broth slowly into the butter and vegetable mixture.
17. Cook uncovered for thirty minutes under medium low heat, stirring frequently so not to burn.
18. Remove bisque from heat.
19. Blend small amounts of bisque in blender and then puree.
20. Puree all of the bisque and pour pureed bisque back into pot with remaining amount.
21. Add chopped lobster meat and heavy cream, heat and serve.
22. If the soup is too thick, thin it by adding milk or water prior to serving.
23. Your dish is ready to be served.

60)   Super Salmon Salad:

Serving: 1

Nutritional Value: 98 calories

Preparation time: 15 minutes

Cook time: 0 minutes

Total time: 15 minutes

Ingredients:

- 80g avocado, stripped, stoned and cut
- 40g celery, cut
- 50g chicory leaves
- 100g smoked salmon cuts
- One huge Medjool date, hollowed and cut
- 20g red onion, cut
- 15g pecans cut
- One tbsp extra-virgin olive oil
- Juice ¼ lemons
- 10g parsley finely cut
- One tbsp capers
- 10g lovage or celery leaves, cut
- 50g arugula leaves

Instructions:

1. Mix the serving of mixed greens leaves on an enormous plate.
2. Combine all the rest of the things and serve on the leaves.
3. Your salad is ready to be served.

61)   Baked Salmon with Mint Dressing:

Serving: 1

Nutritional Value: 340 calories

Preparation time: 10 minutes

Cook time: 10 minutes

Total time: 20 minutes

Ingredients:

- One little bunch (10g) parsley, generally cut
- One salmon filet (130g)
- 40g spinach leaves
- radishes, cut and meagrely cut
- 40g blended serving of mixed greens leaves
- 5cm piece (50g) cucumber, cut into lumps
- Two spring onions, cut

For the dressing:

- Salt and newly ground dark pepper
- 1 tsp low-fat mayonnaise
- 1 tbsp rice vinegar
- 1 tbsp regular yogurt
- Two leaves mint, finely diced

Instructions:

1. Preheat the broiler to 200°C.
2. Place the salmon filet on a heating plate and prepare for 16–18 minutes until simply cooked through. Remove from the broiler and put it in a safe spot. The salmon is similarly decent hot or cold in the plate of mixed greens.
3. If your salmon has skin, basically cook skin side down and expel the salmon from the skin utilizing a fish cut in the wake of cooking. It should slide off effectively when cooked.
4. In a little bowl, combine the mayonnaise, yogurt, rice wine vinegar, mint leaves, and salt and

pepper together and leave for 5 minutes to permit the flavors to create.

5. Arrange the plate of mixed greens leaves and spinach on a serving plate and top with the radishes, cucumber, spring onions, and parsley. Piece the cooked salmon onto the serving of mixed greens and sprinkle the dressing over.

6. Your salad is ready to be served.

62)   Green Salad Skewers:

Serving: 2

Nutritional Value: 306 calories

Preparation time: 30 minutes

Cook time: 10 minutes

Total time: 40 minutes

Ingredients:

- huge dark olives
- wooden sticks, let it absorb water for 30 minutes before use
- 100g feta, cut into eight 3D squares
- ½ red onion cut down the middle and isolated into eight pieces
- cherry tomatoes
- One yellow pepper, cut into eight squares
- 100g cucumber, cut into four cuts and split

For the dressing:

- 1 tsp balsamic vinegar
- 1 tbsp additional virgin olive oil

- ½ clove garlic, stripped and squashed
- Juice of ½ lemon
- Liberal flavoring of salt and newly ground dark pepper
- Not many leaves basil, finely slashed
- ½ tsp dried blended herbs to supplant basil and oregano

Instructions:

1. Thread each stick with the plate of mixed greens things: olive, tomato, yellow pepper, red onion, cucumber, feta, tomato, and olive, yellow pepper, red onion, cucumber.
2. Place all the dressing ingredients in a little bowl and combine completely. Pour over the sticks.
3. Your dish is ready to be served.

63)   Buckwheat Pasta Salad

Serving: 1

Nutritional Value: 112 calories

Preparation time: 10 minutes

Cook time: 0 minutes

Total time: 10 minutes

Ingredients:

- Two cherry tomatoes halved
- A huge bunch of rocket
- A little bunch of basil leaves
- 1/2 avocado, diced

- 20g pine nuts
- Two olives
- 50g buckwheat pasta (cooked as per the bundle instructions)
- One tbsp. additional virgin olive oil

Instructions:

1. Tenderly consolidate all the above mentioned ingredients with the exception of the pine nuts and decorate on a plate or in a bowl
2. Dissipate the pine nuts over the top.
3. Your salad is ready to be served.

64)   Garlic Shrimp Skewers

Preparation time: 10 minutes

Cooking Time: 30 minutes

Serving: 4

Ingredients:

- Worcestershire sauce, one tsp.
- Shrimp, two pound
- Minced garlic, half tsp.
- Butter, two tbsp.
- Lemon juice, half cup
- Wooden skewers
- Salt and Pepper to taste

Instructions:

1. In a medium saucepan melt the butter over medium heat.

2. Add the garlic and sauté for a couple of minutes.
3. Remove from heat.
4. Add lemon juice, Worcestershire sauce, garlic powder, salt, and pepper.
5. Allow the sauce to cool.
6. Reserve half of the sauce in a bowl for brushing.
7. Mix the renaming half of the sauce with the raw shrimp and marinate for thirty minutes.
8. Thread the shrimp onto the wooden skewers.
9. Heat an outdoor grill to medium-high heat.
10. Place the shrimp skewers onto the grill and cook while brushing with the reserved marinade for a few minutes per side or until the shrimp are pink.
11. Your dish is ready to be served.

65)   Shrimp Popcorn

Preparation time: 10 minutes

Cooking Time: 10 minutes

Serving: 4

Ingredients:

- Shrimp, two pound
- Minced garlic, half tsp.
- Milk, two tbsp.
- All- purpose flour, one cup
- Egg, one
- Oil, half cup
- Seasoned salt, one tsp.
- Salt and Pepper to taste

Instructions:

1. Preheat oil to 350 degrees.

2. Combine half cup oil and egg; beat well.
3. Add remaining ingredients except oil for frying and stir until well blended.
4. Dip shrimp into batter to coat.
5. Drop shrimp into hot oil and fry for a few minutes or until golden brown.
6. Remove with slotted spoon; drain on paper towel.
7. Your dish is ready to be served.

66)   Nashville Hot Shrimp

Preparation time: 10 minutes

Cooking Time: 10 minutes

Serving: 4

Ingredients:

- Shrimp, two pound
- Minced garlic, half tsp.
- Milk, two tbsp.
- All- purpose flour, one cup
- Egg, one
- Nashville pepper, three tbsp.
- Oil, half cup
- Seasoned salt, one tsp.
- Salt and Pepper to taste

Instructions:

1. Preheat oil to 350 degrees.
2. Combine half cup oil and egg; beat well.
3. Add remaining ingredients except oil for frying and stir until well blended.
4. Dip shrimp into batter to coat.
5. Drop shrimp into hot oil and fry for a few minutes or until golden brown.

6. Remove with slotted spoon; drain on paper towel.
7. Your dish is ready to be served.

67)   Shrimp Linguini Alfredo

Preparation time: 10 minutes

Cooking Time: 20 minutes

Serving: 4

Ingredients:
- Olive oil, two tbsp.
- Minced garlic, one and a half tsp.
- Flour, one tbsp.
- Butter, four tbsp.
- Heavy cream, two cups
- Parsley, half cup
- Shrimp, half pound
- Salt and pepper to taste
- Parmesan cheese, half cup
- Linguini pasta, one cup

Instructions:
1. Add oil into a pan and then garlic.
2. Add butter, cream and flour and mix until uniform mixture is formed.
3. Add shrimps and cook and then add the linguini pasta.
4. Serve in a bowl with parsley and parmesan cheese on top.

68)   Crab Linguini Pasta

Preparation time: 10 minutes

Cooking Time: 20 minutes

Serving: 4

Ingredients:

- Olive oil, two tbsp.
- Minced garlic, one and a half tsp.
- Flour, one tbsp.
- Butter, four tbsp.
- Heavy cream, two cups
- Parsley, half cup
- Crab meat, half pound
- Salt and pepper to taste
- Parmesan cheese, half cup
- Linguini pasta, one cup

Instructions:

1. Add oil into a pan and then garlic.
2. Add butter, cream and flour and mix until uniform mixture is formed.
3. Add crab meat and cook and then add the linguini pasta.
4. Serve in a bowl with parsley and parmesan cheese on top.

69)   Vegetarian Pizza

Preparation time: 10 minutes

Cooking Time: 30 minutes

Serving: 8

Ingredients:

- Pizza dough, one box
- Garlic powder, half tsp.
- Mushrooms, one cup
- Chili powder, one tsp.
- Olive oil, one tsp.
- Mozzarella cheese, shredded, one cup
- Mixed vegetables, one cup
- Olives, half cup

Instructions:

1. Heat oil in large skillet.
2. Add vegetables and cook, stirring frequently until lightly soft.
3. Stir in seasonings into the mixture.
4. Heat oven to 425 degrees.
5. Sprinkle pizza pan with semolina flour and press dough into pan.

6. Pre-bake dough until it is a very light golden brown, about six minutes.
7. Remove from oven and scatter vegetables, mushrooms, olives on the crust, and top with cheese.
8. Bake for another fifteen minutes until crust is golden brown.
9. Your pizza is ready to be served.

70) Macaroni Salad

Preparation time: 10 minutes

Cooking Time: 10 minutes

Serving: 1

Ingredients:

- Boiled macaroni, as required
- Ketchup, half cup
- Salt and Pepper
- Mayonnaise, half cup
- Powdered sugar, one tbsp.
- Whole milk, a quarter cup
- Sweetened condensed milk, half cup
- Cheddar cheese cubes, one cup
- Pineapple chunks, half cup
- Capsicum, half cup
- Sweet corn, half cup
- Cabbage, half cup

Instructions:

1. Measure all the ingredients in a large salad bowl and mix really well.
2. Chill in fridge for a couple hours before serving.
3. Your dish is ready.

71) Crunchy Thai Salad

Preparation time: 10 minutes

Cooking Time: 10 minutes

Serving: 4

Ingredients:

- Chopped cilantro, 1/4 cup
- Chili Lime Vinaigrette, one tbsp.
- Sweet and Spicy Peanut Sauce, one tbsp.
- Shredded red cabbage, one cup
- Medium carrots peeled and shredded, two
- Shelled edamame, half cup
- Sliced almonds toasted, half cup
- Wonton Strips
- Napa or Savory cabbage chopped, half cup
- Fresh spinach coarsely chopped, two cups
- Green onions thinly sliced, three

For Frying the Shrimps:

- Butter, half tsp.
- Olive oil, two tbsp.
- Chili powder, half tsp.
- Cayenne pepper, half tsp.
- Minced garlic, one tsp.
- Raw shrimp peeled and deveined, eight ounces

Instructions:

1. In a large self-sealing plastic bag, combine shrimp, minced garlic, chili powder, and cayenne.
2. Toss until shrimps are evenly coated with the spice mix.
3. Heat a large, heavy skillet over medium high heat. Melt olive oil and butter and swirl to coat the bottom of the skillet.
4. Add shrimps in a single layer. Pan-fry for about 2 minutes, then turn and fry until shrimps become pink all the way through and slightly firm, about 2-3 minutes. Do not overcook the shrimps.
5. Carefully remove from skillet and set aside.
6. Assemble the salad.
7. Layer or toss cabbages, spinach, carrots, edamame, green onions, and sliced almonds, wonton strips, and cilantro in bowl.
8. Serve with Chili-Lime Vinaigrette and Sweet & Spicy Peanut Sauce.
9. Garnish with additional cilantro and wonton strips.

72) Double Crunch Shrimp

Preparation Time: 10 minutes

Cooking Time: 10 minutes

Serving: 2-3

Ingredients:

For Sauce:
- Chili bean paste, two tbsp.
- Chili paste, one tsp.
- Cornstarch, one tsp.
- Chicken broth, half cup
- Oyster sauce, two tbsp.
- Sherry, half cup

For Shrimps:
- Salt and pepper, to taste
- Seasoning salt, to taste
- Oil, for cooking
- Water, two tbsp.
- Panko, one cup
- Flour, one cup
- Shrimp, one and a half pounds
- Eggs, two

Instructions:

1. Use the shrimps by cutting vertically down the back of the shrimp. Leave tails on.
2. Season shrimp with salt, pepper, and seasoning salt.
3. Heat enough oil to deep fry the shrimp in a skillet to 350 degrees.
4. Put panko crumbs in a shallow dish. Add seasonings to taste and mix well.
5. Put flour in a separate shallow dish.
6. Beat the eggs and water together.
7. Dip the shrimps in the egg-water mixture.
8. Add the shrimps to the flour.
9. Dip again in egg-water mixture.
10. Toss shrimps in panko crumbs.
11. Fry in hot oil at 350 degrees F until golden, about 3 minutes.

12.   Drain the fried shrimps on the cooling racks over paper towels.
13.   In a large pot mix together all of the ingredients for the sauce, making sure that the cornstarch dissolves thoroughly.
14.   Heat a wok or large skillet on high heat with a teaspoon of oil.
15.   Add the sauce and let it simmer for 1 minute to thicken. Add the shrimps, toss to coat, and simmer for 1 more minute.
16.   Your crunchy shrimps are ready to serve.

73)   California Roll

Preparation Time: 15 minutes

Cooking Time: 30 minutes

Serving: 4

Ingredients:

- Rice vinegar, quarter cup
- Granulated sugar, two tbsp.
- Salt, half tsp.
- White rice, two cups
- Water, two cups

For Sriracha Mayo Crab:

- Light mayonnaise, a quarter cup
- Sriracha, two tbsp.
- Crab meat, twelve ounces

For Toppings:

- Julienned carrots
- Large avocado
- English cucumber, (thinly sliced)

Instructions:

1. Add the rice to a fine mesh strainer, and run under cold water for 1-2 minutes, rinsing until the water runs clear.
2. Allow the rice to thoroughly drain, and then transfer it to a medium saucepan with two cups of water.
3. Place on high heat and bring the rice to a boil.
4. Once boiling, reduce the heat to low, and cover with a lid. Simmer 15 minutes. Remove from heat and allow to rest, undisturbed, and covered, for 15 additional minutes.
5. While you wait, place a small nonstick pan over medium heat.
6. Add the rice vinegar, sugar, and salt. Cook, stirring with a whisk, until the sugar has dissolved completely.
7. Remove from the burner to allow to cool down slightly.
8. When the rice is ready, pour the vinegar mixture over the top of the rice, and stir to thoroughly mix.
9. Fold until all of the vinegar mixture has been absorbed by the rice.
10. To a small mixing bowl, combine the crab meat with the sriracha, and mayonnaise. Mix well.
11. In four bowls add the rice and layer with crab mixture, cucumber slices, carrots, diced avocado, sesame seeds, and micro greens.
12. Drizzle with soy sauce, and serve right away.

74)   Dragon Roll

Preparation time: 15 minutes

Cooking Time: 60 minutes

Serving: 4

Ingredients:

- Lemon, half
- Nori sheets, two
- Sushi rice, two cups
- Shrimp tempura, eight pieces
- Tobiko, two tbsp.
- Unagi (eel)
- Persian/Japanese cucumbers, one
- Avocados, one

Instructions:

1. Gather all the ingredients.
2. Cut cucumber lengthwise into quarters.
3. Remove the seeds, and then cut in half lengthwise.
4. Cut the avocado in half lengthwise around the seed, and twist the two halves until they separate.
5. Hack the knife edge into the pit. Hold the skin of the avocado with the other hand, and twist in counter directions.
6. Remove the skin, and slice the avocado widthwise.
7. Gently presses the avocados slices with your fingers, and then keep pressing gently, and evenly with the side of the knife until the length of avocado is about the length of sushi roll.
8. Wrap the bamboo mat with plastic wrap, and place half of the nori sheet, shiny side down.

9. Turn it over and put the shrimp tempura, cucumber strips, and tobiko at the bottom end of the nori sheet.
10. If you like to put unagi, place it inside here as well.
11. From the bottom end, start rolling nori sheet over the filling tightly, and firmly with bamboo mat until the bottom end reaches the nori sheet.
12. Place the bamboo mat over the roll and tightly squeeze the roll.
13. Using the side of the knife, place the avocado on top of the roll.
14. Place plastic wrap over the roll and then put the bamboo mat over.
15. Cut the roll into 8 pieces with the knife.
16. Put tobiko on each piece of sushi, and drizzle spicy mayo, and sprinkle black sesame seeds on top.
17. Your dish is ready to be served.

75)   Cobb Salad

Preparation Time: 10 minutes

Total Time: 10 minutes

Serving: 4

Ingredients:

- Cucumber, peeled and cubed, half cup
- Cherry tomatoes, cut in half
- Garbanzo beans, rinsed, one cup
- Cooked quinoa, a quarter cup
- Slivered almonds, three tbsp.
- Sunflower seeds to sprinkle on top
- Cracked pepper
- Romaine Lettuce, two

- Asparagus spears, cut, four grilled
- Green beans, cut, half cup
- Cubed roasted golden beets, half cup
- Avocado, cubed, half

Instructions:

1. Place cut Romaine lettuce on plate.
2. Place all cut vegetables in sections on the salad greens.
3. Mix the quinoa with the slivered almonds and place quinoa in the middle of the salad.
4. Drizzle your preferred dressing on top and serve.

4.4 Recipes for Juices, Sweet Dishes and Snacks

76)   Muesli

Ingredients:

- 100g strawberries, hulled and diced
- 10g buckwheat puffs
- 15g coconut drops or dried up coconut
- 20g buckwheat cereal
- 40g Medjool dates, hollowed and diced
- 10g cocoa nibs
- 15g pecans, diced
- 100g plain Greek yogurt (or vegetarian type, for example, soya or coconut yogurt)

Instructions:

1. Blend the entire of the above things together.
2. Possibly including the yogurt and strawberries before serving before making it in mass.
3. Your dish is ready to be served.

77) Banana Blueberry Pancakes with Apple Compote and Turmeric Latte

Serving: 2

Nutritional Value: 105 calories

Preparation time: 13 minutes

Cook time: 10 minutes

Total time: 23 minutes

Ingredients:

For preparing the Pancakes

- 225g blueberries
- Six bananas
- 150g oats

- Six eggs
- Two tsp baking powder
- ¼ teaspoon salt

For preparing the Apple Compote

- 1/4 teaspoon cinnamon powder
- Two apples
- One tablespoon lemon juice
- Five dates (pitted)
- salt to taste

For preparing the Turmeric Latte

- stripped ginger root
- One teaspoon turmeric powder
- Touch of dark pepper (expands ingestion)
- One teaspoon cinnamon powder
- Three cups of coconut milk
- One teaspoon crude nectar
- Touch of cayenne pepper (discretionary)

Instructions:

1. Put the oats in a rapid blender and let it grind for one moment or until an oat flour has framed. You should ensure that your blender is dry before doing this, or probably everything will get spongy.
2. Presently include the bananas, eggs, heating powder and salt to the blender and grind for 2 minutes until a smooth mixture structures.
3. Move the blend to an enormous bowl and overlay in the blueberries. Leave to rest for 10 mins while the baking powder actuates.
4. To make your cakes, include a bit of margarine to your skillet on a medium-high stove. Include a

couple of spoons of the blueberry cake blend and fry for until pleasantly brilliant on the base side. Hurl the flapjack to sear the opposite side.

5. Remove the center and flat cleave your apples.
6. Pop everything in a food processor, along with two tablespoons of water and a touch of salt. Grind it to shape your stout apple compote.
7. Mix all the things in a rapid blender until smooth.
8. Fill it in a little container and warm for 4 minutes over a medium stove until hot yet not bubbling.
9. Your pancakes are ready to be served along with your latte.

78)   Fish and Chips

Preparation Time: 10 minutes

Cooking Time: 10 minutes

Serving: 2-4

Ingredients:

- Large russet potatoes, peeled and cut lengthwise, four
- All-purpose flour, two cups
- Seafood seasoning, two tsp.
- Kosher salt, according to taste
- Peanut or vegetable oil, for frying
- Baking soda, one tsp.
- Cold beer, one bottle
- Haddock fillets, skinned and cut diagonally, two pounds

Instructions:

1. Warm the oil in a large pot over medium stove.

2. Heat the oil to 325 degrees.
3. Control the temperature with a treats thermometer.
4. Keep the potato sticks in a bowl of water to maintain the color of the potatoes before cooking.
5. Fry the potatoes until they are cooked through and delicate yet have no shading, around four to five minutes.
6. Delicately move the spoon around as the fries are cooking. Take them off from the oil and put them promptly on a paper towel lined heating sheet.
7. Preheat the stove to 300 degrees and raise the temperature of the cooking oil to 375 degrees.
8. In a medium bowl, mix the flour, seasoning, and touch of salt.
9. At the point when the oil is preheated to the right temperature.
10. Coat the fish liberally.
11. While adding the fish to the oil, plunge half of the filet into the oil and permit the blender to begin puffing, and afterward delicately slide it into the oil.
12. Fry the fish until they are brilliantly earthy colored and firm, around 5 minutes turning the fish over, during the cooking time.
13. Move the fish to a serving platter, and present with the fries.

79)   Green Juice

Ingredients:

- One medium pear, cut into eighths
- stems of celery
- One medium green apple, cut into eighths
- 1/2 huge cucumber, cut into quarters

Instructions:

1. Squeeze all the things adhering to the directions for ordinary squeezing in your juicer manual.
2. Drink quickly, or let chill for an hour and enjoy later.

80)   Chocolate and Coffee Mousse

Serving: 8

Nutritional Value: 242 calories

Preparation time: 4 hours

Cook time: 15 minutes

Total time: 4 hours and 15 minutes

Ingredients:

- Cinnamon 1/2 tsp 300 ml of Almond milk
- Cocoa powder 2 tbsp.
- Espresso 200 ml
- Gelatin powder 1 tbsp.
- Coconut yogurt 300 g
- Maple syrup 2 tbsp.
- Chocolate unadulterated 200 g

Instructions:

1. Join the almond milk and espresso in a pan and sprinkle the gelatin over it. Let it be for 5 minutes.
2. Mix the blend well and bring to bubble quickly. At that point, quickly remove the container from the stove.
3. Mix the maple syrup, cinnamon, and the dim chocolate into the hot fluid. Keep on blending until the chocolate has totally dissolved and has been assimilated into the blend.
4. Pour it in enriching pastry glasses and let it set in the refrigerator for approximately 4 hours.
5. Prior to serving, decorate with a spoon of coconut yogurt and residue with cocoa.
6. Your dish is ready to be served.

81)   Melon and Grape Juice

Serving: 2

Nutritional Value: 125 calories

Preparation time: 2 minutes

Cook time: 0 minutes

Total time: 2 minutes

Ingredients:

- 100g melon, stripped, deseeded and cut into pieces
- ½ cucumber, stripped however liked, split, seeds evacuated and diced
- 100g red seedless grapes
- 30g small spinach leaves, stalk less

Instructions:

1. Blend together all the things in a blender and pour it out in glasses.
2. Serve your juice right away.

82)   Black Current and Kale Smoothie

Serving: 2

Nutritional Value: 186 calories

Preparation time: 4 minutes

Cook time: 0 minutes

Total time: 4 minutes

Ingredients:

- One banana
- One tsp nectar
- One cup newly made green tea
- Five ice 3D shapes
- kale leaves, stalk less
- 40 g blackcurrants, washed

Instructions:

1. Mix the nectar into the warm green tea until properly mixed.
2. Prodigy all the things together in a blender until smooth.
3. Serve right away.

83)   Green Tea Smoothie

Serving: 2

Nutritional Value: 183 calories

Preparation time: 3 minutes

Cook time: 0 minutes

Total time: 3 minutes

Ingredients:

- Two tsp matcha green tea powder
- Two bananas
- 250 ml of milk
- Three tsp nectar
- 1/2 tsp vanilla bean
- Five ice 3D squares

Instructions:

1. Basically, mix all the things together in a blender and serve in two glasses.
2. Drink it without storing it for later.

84)   Black current and Raspberry Jelly

Serving: 2

Nutritional Value: 76 calories

Preparation time: 2 minutes

Cook time: 15 minutes

Total time: 17 minutes

Ingredients:

- Two tbsp. granulated sugar
- 100g raspberries washed
- 100g blackcurrants washed
- 300ml water
- Two packs gelatin

Instructions:

1. Arrange the raspberries in two serving dishes/glasses/molds. Put the gelatin in a bowl of cold water to mollify.
2. Place the blackcurrants in a little skillet with the sugar and 100ml water and bring to bubble. Stew enthusiastically for 5 minutes and afterward remove it from the heat. Leave it in the open for 2 minutes.
3. Squeeze out abundant water from the gelatin leaves and add them to the pan. Mix until completely mixed, at that point mix in the remainder of the water. Empty the fluid into the readied dishes and refrigerate to set. These ought to be prepared in around 3-4 hours or overnight.
4. Your jelly after setting is ready to be served.

85)   Chocolate Bites:

Ingredients:

- 250g Medjool dates pitted
- 30g dull chocolate broken into pieces; or cocoa nibs
- 1 tbsp cocoa powder
- 120g pecans

- 1 tbsp ground turmeric
- 1 tbsp additional virgin olive oil
- 1–2 tbsp water
- 1 tsp vanilla concentrate

Instructions:

1. Put the pecans and chocolate in a food processor and keep it processing until you have a fine powder.
2. Include the various things with the exception of the water and mix until the blend shapes a ball. You could conceivably need to include the water depending on the consistency of the blend. You don't need it to be excessively clingy.
3. Utilizing your hands, structure the blend into scaled-down balls, and refrigerate in a hermetically sealed compartment for approximately one hour before eating them.
4. You could move a portion of the balls in some more cocoa or dried up a coconut to accomplish an alternate completion if you like.
5. They can be stored up for a week.
6. Your dish is ready to be served.
7. Enjoy your meal.

86)   Banana and Chocolate Smoothie

Preparation time: 5 minutes

Serving: 1

Ingredients:

- Frozen banana chunks, ½ cup
- Frozen chocolate chunks, ½ cup
- Peanut Butter ice cream, one scoop
- Low fat milk, one cup

Instructions:

1. Add all the ingredients in a blender and blend appropriately for three to four minutes.
2. Now pour into a cup and enjoy.
3. You can store this smoothie by freezing it.
4. Prior to using it later, you can re-blend the smoothie.

87)   Mango and Pineapple Smoothie

Preparation time: 5 minutes

Serving: 1

Ingredients:

- Frozen mango chunks, ½ cup
- Frozen Pineapple chunks, ½ cup
- Vanilla ice cream, one scoop
- Low fat milk, one cup

Instructions:

1. Add all the ingredients in a blender and blend appropriately for three to four minutes.

2. Now pour into a cup and enjoy.

3. You can store this smoothie by freezing it.

4. Prior to using it later, you can re-blend the smoothie.

88)   Superfood Smoothie

Preparation time: 5 minutes

Serving: 1

Ingredients:

- Frozen kiwi chunks, ½ cup
- Fresh spinach, ½ cup
- Cucumber chunks, ¼ cup
- Chia seeds, one tsp.
- Low fat almond milk, one cup
- Vanilla protein powder, ½ cup

Instructions:

1. Add all the ingredients in a blender and blend appropriately for three to four minutes.

2. Now pour into a cup and enjoy.

3. You can store this smoothie by freezing it.

4. Prior to using it later, you can re-blend the smoothie.

89) Greek Yoghurt and Berry Smoothie

Preparation time: 5 minutes

Serving: 1

Ingredients:
- Frozen berries chunks, ½ cup
- Frozen Greek yoghurt, ½ cup
- Peanut Butter ice cream, one scoop
- Low fat almond milk, one cup
- Vanilla protein powder, ½ cup

Instructions:
1. Add all the ingredients in a blender and blend appropriately for three to four minutes.
2. Now pour into a cup and enjoy.
3. You can store this smoothie by freezing it.
4. Prior to using it later, you can re-blend the smoothie.

90) Apple Pie Smoothie

Preparation time: 5 minutes

Serving: 1

Ingredients:

- Frozen apple chunks, peeled, ½ cup
- Vanilla extract, one tsp.
- Cinnamon powder, ¼ tsp.
- Nutmeg powder, ¼ tsp.
- Low fat milk, one cup

Instructions:

1. Add all the ingredients in a blender and blend appropriately for three to four minutes.
2. Now pour into a cup and enjoy.
3. You can store this smoothie by freezing it.
4. Prior to using it later, you can re-blend the smoothie.

91)   Red Berries Smoothie

Preparation time: 5 minutes

Serving: 1

Ingredients:

- Frozen red berries chunks, ½ cup
- Vanilla protein powder, ½ cup
- Low fat milk, one cup

Instructions:

1. Add all the ingredients in a blender and blend appropriately for three to four minutes.
2. Now pour into a cup and enjoy.

3. You can store this smoothie by freezing it.

4. Prior to using it later, you can re-blend the smoothie.

92)   Pear and Banana Protein Smoothie

Preparation time: 5 minutes

Serving: 1

Ingredients:
- Frozen banana chunks, ½ cup
- Vanilla protein powder, ½ cup
- Low fat milk, one cup
- Frozen Pear chunks, ½ cup

Instructions:
1. Add all the ingredients in a blender and blend appropriately for three to four minutes.
2. Now pour into a cup and enjoy.
3. You can store this smoothie by freezing it.
4. Prior to using it later, you can re-blend the smoothie.

93)   Tomato Smoothie

Preparation time: 5 minutes

Serving: 1

Ingredients:

- Lemon juice, two tbsp.
- Carrot juice, ½ cup
- Tomato juice, one cup
- Tomatoes peeled, ½ cup
- Celery Stalk chopped, one

Instructions:

1. Add all the ingredients in a blender and blend appropriately for three to four minutes.
2. Now pour into a cup and enjoy.
3. You can store this smoothie by freezing it.
4. Prior to using it later, you can re-blend the smoothie.

94)   Red Velvet Cake

Preparation Time: 15 minutes

Cooking Time: 35 minutes

Serving: 12

Ingredients:

- Cocoa powder, two cups
- Buttermilk, one cup
- Large eggs, two
- Food color, red
- All-purpose flour, two cups
- Salt, one tsp.

- Vanilla essence, one tsp.
- Vinegar, one tbsp.
- Baking soda, one tsp.
- Shortening, half cup
- Sugar, one and a half cup
- Butter, half cup

Instructions:

1. Cream butter and sugar; add eggs and blend.
2. Add food coloring, water, and cocoa.
3. Blend in buttermilk; add flour and salt gradually.
4. Add vanilla and beat until mixed. Mix vinegar and soda and stir in last; do not beat.
5. Pour into two nine- inch pans.
6. Bake for 30 to 35 minutes in a 350 degree oven. Frost with fluff frosting.
7. Add milk mixture and vanilla; continue beating.
8. When icing is very fluffy, frost cool cake.

95)   Double Chocolate Smoothie

Preparation time: 5 minutes

Serving: 1

Ingredients:

- Frozen Greek Yoghurt, ½ cup
- Unsweetened Cocoa powder, ¼ tsp.
- Banana chunks, ¼ tsp.
- Chocolate protein powder, ¼ cup
- Low fat milk, one cup

Instructions:

1. Add all the ingredients in a blender and blend appropriately for three to four minutes.
2. Now pour into a cup and enjoy.
3. You can store this smoothie by freezing it.
4. Prior to using it later, you can re-blend the smoothie.

96)   Stout Irish Cream Cake

Preparation Time: 15 minutes

Cooking Time: 45 minutes

Serving: 12

Ingredients:

- Irish cream Liqueur, half cup
- Cream cheese, eight ounce
- Sugar, five cups
- Butter, one cup
- Stuat beer, one cup
- Sour cream, one cup
- Eggs, two
- All-purpose flour, one cup
- Vanilla essence, one tsp.
- Cocoa powder, half cup

Instructions:
1. Mix all the ingredients together and bake for 40 minutes approximately.
2. Dust sugar on top and serve.

97) Pumpkin Spice Smoothie

Preparation time: 5 minutes

Serving: 1

Ingredients:
- Frozen pumpkin puree, ½ cup
- Cinnamon powder, ¼ tsp.
- Ground ginger powder, ¼ tsp.
- Ground cloves powder, ¼ tsp.
- Decaffeinated Coffee, ¾ cup
- Vanilla protein powder, 1/4cup

- Low fat milk, one cup

Instructions:

1. Add all the ingredients in a blender and blend appropriately for three to four minutes.
2. Now pour into a cup and enjoy.
3. You can store this smoothie by freezing it.
4. Prior to using it later, you can re-blend the smoothie.

98)   Artichoke and Spinach Dip

Preparation time: 5 minutes

Cooking Time: 35 minutes

Serving: 10

Ingredients:

- Cream cheese, eight ounces
- Artichoke, ten ounces
- Garlic Alfredo sauce, sixteen ounces
- Chopped spinach, ten ounces
- Mozzarella cheese, shredded, two cups
- Parmesan and cheddar cheese mix, shredded, one cup

Instructions:

1. Mix all ingredients in a large bowl.
2. Pour into crock pot and set on high for 35 minutes.
3. Your dip is ready to serve.

99)   Original Cheesecake

Preparation Time: 10 minutes

Cooking Time: 10 minutes

Serving: 5

Ingredients:

- Sour cream, half cup
- Large eggs, five
- Vanilla extract, two tsp.
- Graham crackers, one and a half cup
- Ground Cinnamon, half tsp.
- Butter, half cup
- Sugar, one and a half cup

Instructions:

1. Use an electric mixer to mix cream cheese, sugar, sour cream and vanilla and cinnamon.
2. Blend until smooth and creamy.
3. Scrape down sides of bowl.
4. Whisk eggs in a bowl; add to cream cheese mixture. Blend just until eggs are incorporated.
5. Add the graham cracker layer which is made by combining butter and graham crackers together first and then the cream cheese mixture.
6. Freeze the mixture for one hour and serve with sour cream on top.

100) Chocolate Frosties

Preparation Time: 5 minutes

Cooking Time: 10 minutes

Serving: 4

Ingredients:

- Milk, one cup
- Vanilla ice-cream, four scoops
- Chocolate milk powder, eight tbsp.

Instructions:

1. Allow the ice cream to soften just enough to blend easily
2. Mix everything thoroughly in a blender.
3. Once everything is thoroughly combined, mix until you have reached the desired softness.
4. Serve right away in glasses, with spoons.

All the recipes mentioned in this chapter are easy to make by yourself at home.

Conclusion

Our daily life revolves around our busy schedules. In this routine, finding something healthy to eat becomes less of a priority especially for individuals that work vigorously to earn for their families. In such conditions, health is compromised to a greater extent that can cause many side effects in the future. To avoid such conditions it is very important to not only eat healthy but also to eat right.

This book covers the life of a Pescatarian, making it easy for them to prepare their favorite recipes inside their kitchen without any stress. This book explains how a Pescatarian diet differs from other diets and how it can be beneficial to a human being who wants to lose weight while eating healthy food.

Being a Pescatarian is no more boring or difficult with all these amazing breakfast, lunch, dinner, snacks, juices, and sweets recipes mentioned in this book. You will also get a seven day diet plan that you can change according to your taste and preferences with the variety of recipes mentioned in the book. So, there is no need to wait more when you can cook healthy and yummy right in your home.

Made in United States
Troutdale, OR
12/02/2023

15245741R00131